Jan Morris was born in 1926 of a Welsh father and an English mother, and when she is not travelling she lives with her partner Elizabeth Morris in the top left-hand corner of Wales, between the mountains and the sea.

Her books include *Coronation Everest*, *Venice*, The *Pax Britannica* Trilogy (*Heaven's Command*, *Pax Britannica*, and *Farewell the Trumpets*), and *Conundrum*. She is also the author of six books about cities and countries, two autobiographical books, several volumes of collected travel essays and the unclassifiable *Trieste and the Meaning of Nowhere*. *A Writer's World*, a collection of her travel writing and reportage from over five decades, was published in 2003. *Hav*, her novel, was published in a new and expanded form in 2006. Her most recent book, *Contact!*, about the people she encountered on her many travels, was published in 2009.

by the same author

JAN MORRIS

Manhattan '45

faber and faber

First published in 1987
This new edition published in 2011
by Faber and Faber Limited
Bloomsbury House
74–77 Great Russell Street
London WC1B 3DA

Printed in England by CPI Bookmarque, Croydon

All rights reserved
© Jan Morris, 1987, 2011

The right of Jan Morris to be identified as author of this work
has been asserted in accordance with Section 77 of the
Copyright, Designs and Patents Act 1988

A CIP record for this book
is available from the British Library

ISBN 978–0–571–24178–1

2 4 6 8 10 9 7 5 3 1

Dedicated to the Memory of

PFC. PETER P. GELZINIS
PFC. FRED M. GHENTS
S./SGT. MARTIN LIEBENHAUT
PVT. KENT A. RANDOLPH
PFC. MICHAEL J. RATCHFORD
2ND LT. JEAN J. SCHIFF
CAPT. RICHARD V. SOUTHWELL
PFC. HARRY STUART
SGT. STEPHEN F. WHITE

Contents

vii

CONTENTS

A New Introduction

This book, which describes the island-city of Manhattan at the apex of its splendour, is attended by sadness now, more than half a century later. In 1945, in a world so recently wracked and impoverished by war, New Yorkers thought themselves uniquely fortunate, citizens of a town that was beyond all doubt the glittering apex of western civilization. It was immensely rich, it was full of gifted people, it was powerful, it was fun, and it was the talisman of a nation that could do anything.

Since then New York's status in the world has been diminished. The United States of America is no longer the single superpower of the planet, and Manhattan is no longer unique in its glitter and its pride. In 2001 hostile foreigners deliberately flew aeroplanes into its tallest buildings, killing thousands of citizens, and this was not only a tragedy for the city, it was a humiliation too. It is perhaps sadly true to say that the civic spirit has never been quite so buoyant since, and the twin towers of the World Trade Center, once the two tallest on earth, have long since been overtaken by taller structures in lesser cities far away.

So this book, although I hope its flavour properly represents the exuberant flair of Manhattan in 1945, necessarily has elegiac undertones – we all know what was to happen to it. But by now it has recovered much of its serenity, much of its merriment too, and I like to think that those of us who love the magnificent old place, in its pride as in its pathos, in reading about its character of not so long ago will feel that they are also reading about its character now.

Jan Morris
2011

Prologue

In the early afternoon of June 20, 1945, the grey-painted British liner *Queen Mary*, 80,774 tons, appeared out of a misty sea at the Narrows, the entrance to the harbor of New York City. She was the second largest ship in the world, and probably the most famous, and she was bringing home to the United States 14,526 of the American service men and women who had just helped to win the war against Nazi Germany—the first big contingent to return from the great victory. As she sailed past Sandy Hook the resonant boom of her foghorn, which sounded a note two octaves below middle A, echoed away triumphantly to Brooklyn, to the New Jersey waterfront, and past the Statue of Liberty to the waiting skyscrapers.

The ship was welcomed like a promise of great times. Overhead flew a U.S. Navy dirigible; trailing the liner gamely up the Narrows were an elderly railroad steamer full of pressmen, and two requisitioned motor yachts full of girls—with a Women's Air Corps band thumping away on one of them, and the girls, flowers in their hair, jitterbugging on deck to whistles and ribaldry from the soldiers crowding every inch of rail, every porthole of the liner high above.[1] When she entered the wide expanse of New York Bay, treading easily towards the city with only a gentle sliver of steam from her funnels, flotillas of lesser vessels came out to greet her, milled about her passage or hastily got out of her way— a couple of aircraft carriers, many tugs, freighters, tall-funnelled ferryboats, sludge barges, train-flats, launches and lighters of every kind, the 16-knot fireboat *The Firefighter*, most powerful in the world, enthusiastically spouting its water plumes. All around the waterfront, on every wharf and every vantage point, crowds were waving; hundreds of cars jammed the Brooklyn shore road, and the passing Staten Island ferries listed to port or starboard, according to passage, with the weight of their cheering passengers.

On the bridge of the liner stood her captain, Commodore Sir James Bissett, one of the best-known

---

[1] They had been selected by Captain Henry E. Astheimer, Co-ordinator of Morale Activities at the port's military headquarters, who said he had a waiting list of about five thousand ready to greet later troopships.

4

of the Atlantic shipmasters, and the Sandy Hook pilot, Mr. Wilmur J. Crocker. Jamming the decks below, so tightly they could hardly move, and those in the middle of the ship could see nothing whatever of the passing spectacle, 14,000 Americans sang, shouted, waved in all directions, brandished slogans ("Cheerioh Agnes," "We Made It Mom"), released blown-up condoms like balloons, wolf-whistled at the bandswomen (fast falling astern as they swung into "Don't Fence Me In"), blew trumpets, swapped wisecracks, just stood meditatively thinking, or in the case of one female lieutenant nurse, waved a pair of black lace panties out of a porthole. A hundred ships' sirens bellowed, whistled or grunted across the bay. Half a million hands fluttered. Five docking tugs pushed their way alongside. *The Firefighter* lavishly erupted—20,000 gallons of water a minute.

And ahead of them there waited the towers of the city, clustered on their narrow island, glittering in the afternoon sun. Soldiers on the port side of the ship could not see them, only the Statue of Liberty, Ellis Island and the low drab outline of the New Jersey shore, but to the thousands on the starboard side those towers were a pledge of home and happiness. Untouched by the war the men had left behind them, they stood there metal-clad, steel-ribbed, glass-shrouded, colossal and romantic—everything that America seemed to represent in a world of loss and ruin. Fleets of merchant ships lay at the island's 103 piers. Clouds of steam arose among its buildings. Down every cross-street, as the liner moved carefully up the Hudson River, a multitudinous traffic could be glimpsed, very unlike the austere or dilapidated traffic of Europe—gleaming, bright-painted traffic, endlessly energetic and confident. Flags flew everywhere. Windows flashed. A vast dull city roar sounded behind the raucous sirens. "Welcome Home," said a gigantic sign painted on an oil tank. "Welcome Home," said a banner draped on a pleasure-steamer. "Welcome Home," shouted the tug captains through their bull-horns.

By evening the *Queen Mary* was being warped into Pier 90 on the West Side, and the soldiers at the rail were cheerfully booing the military policemen lined up on the quay for their reception. Red Cross ladies were there too, their trestle tables laden with 35,000 half-pint containers of milk provided by the National Dairy Products Corporation, and civic dignitaries with button-holes, and military bigwigs bright with decorations, and coveys of photographers in snap-brim fedora hats. Slowly, slowly the ship was eased alongside. "Hey," shouted a G.I. to the waiting pressmen, "What town is this?"

THE TOWN was Manhattan, the core island of New York. Its approximate center, in the middle of Central Park, lay at latitude 40°46′56″ N, longitude 73°57′57″ W. It was the town of all towns, and this was a culminating moment of its history. Though another two months were to pass before the victory over Japan and the end of the Second World War, Manhattan already knew

itself to be entering a splendid fulfillment. This was
not only bound to be, in the postwar years, the supreme
and symbolical American city. All the signs were that
it would be the supreme city of the Western world, or
even the world as a whole. New York in 1945 saw itself,
said a publicity booklet issued by the Bankers' Trust
Company (corner of Wall and Nassau Streets), as repre-
senting a people "to whom nothing is impossible."

And indeed to everyone who went there, in the
months after the docking of the *Queen Mary* that day,
the feeling that nothing was beyond the civic potential
was an inescapable part of the atmosphere. This small
island, 14,000 acres in area, 12½ miles from top to
bottom, 2½ miles wide at its widest point, 268 feet
above the sea at its highest ground level, 1.9 million
in population—this crowded island was the head, the
brain, the essence of America, and the idea of America
was omnipotent then. The Manhattan skyline shim-
mered in the imaginations of all the nations, and
people everywhere cherished the ambition, however
unattainable, of landing one day upon that legendary
foreshore, where the sirens always hooted, the bright
lights perpetually shone, and black lace panties dangled
emblematically from portholes. The flash and merriment of it was like a tonic, to the fancy of a debilitated
world. Its wealth, contemplated with as much wonder
as envy by less advantaged societies everywhere, seemed
to show that every populace *might* be rich. Seen in
magazine photographs, in propaganda leaflets, or in the
backgrounds of Hollywood musicals, Manhattan looked

all panache, all rhythm, all good-natured dazzle, all Frank Sinatra and Betty Grable. It was the Present tantalizingly sublimated. It was the Future about to occur.

That Bankers' Trust booklet was bursting with momentous projects. New Yorkers, it conceded, were not supermen, just ordinary people trying to do a good job in the American way, but the tone of the text was all-confident nevertheless. "New York Means Business," announced its first chapter heading, and on rich thick paper it went on to describe what was about to happen in the city, now that the war was over—huge new housing projects, the largest bus terminal in the world, an airport eight times as big as the one they had already, an immense new sports center, terrific new museums, huge new hotels, lavish new nightclubs, skyscraper offices, department stores, dozens of new schools, marvellous new hospitals, roads, tunnels, piers, parks, markets, truck terminals, telephone systems, TV transmitters, radio relay stations, a magnificent new civic center. During the next few heady years the city was going to have to buy 148 million board feet of lumber, 22 million barrels of cement, 440 million bricks, 1.30 million tons of steel, 263,573 doors and 11,648,000 square yards of asphalt paving surface, besides nearly a million new automobiles. This was more than mere speculation. There was no doubt about it. "New York has made up its mind . . . New York won't wait."

Everywhere, emblazoned across the city by its own unrivalled advertising industry, were the signs of boom times coming, after all the restraints and restrictions of the war, and the Great Depression that had preceded it. A million new cars? The dealers were ready. "The news on Mercury is plenty good. It will be a big car, sturdy and eager for Action. Quick on the pick-up, and smooth. . . ." A new airport? "You won't have to wait for improvements in personal planes—they'll be waiting for you in the post-war ERCOUPE, the certified spin-proof plane!" 440 million bricks, 1.30 million tons of steel? Never worry—"THE ERIE RAILROAD IS READY TO GO." According to the Director of War Mobilization and Reconversion, who had recently reported on economic prospects to the President and Congress, Americans now faced the pleasant predicament of having to learn how to live 50 percent better than they had ever lived before.

Nor was this simply a return to the good old days before the Wall Street crash. The war had made America rich in a new kind. During the past two wartime years the average citizen had been able to save a quarter of his income, and by June 1945 the liquid assets of the people, at $140 billion, totalled three times the entire national income in 1932—all in all, it is said, a quarter of a trillion dollars was waiting to be spent on consumer goods. At the same time the decisions of the Bretton Woods financial conference, in 1944, had made it certain that the U.S. dollar would be the master-currency of the postwar world. America was realizing its stupendous strength, and as a result New York was emerging from a provincial, even a parochial sort of urbanity into true metropolitanism. The old brag "biggest and finest in the nation" more and more evolved into "biggest and finest in the world," and already lobbyists were arguing that Manhattan was the only logical site for the new league of States, the United Nations.

Battered and impoverished London, humiliated Paris, shattered Berlin, discredited Rome—the old capitals towards which, before the war, Americans had so often looked with sensations of diffident inferiority, now seemed flaccid beside this prodigy of the West; visitors from abroad, who in former times had generally responded to New York with a sort of spellbound condescension, could hardly patronize Manhattan now. There seemed a momentous symbolism to the very stance of the place, and Manhattan was its own best logo: unmistakable, unforgettable, and conveying messages, as Madison Avenue would wish it, altogether seductive. How marvellous, that the hopes of mankind should be illustrated by an emblem so gloriously exuberant!

It had its sad and seamy sides, its poverty and its greed, its ugliness and its dirt; but inasmuch as a city can ever live up to its popular reputation, or its own self-image, Manhattan did so in the months immediately after the victory in Europe. The dropping of the first nuclear bombs on Japan, which seemed to have made America invincible, heightened the city's sense of destiny. The miserable aftermath of war, almost everywhere else in the world, only made it the more resplendent in contrast. Ask almost anyone who remembers Manhattan then, and they recall it with proud nostalgia, even if they were poor and lonely; and if their memories have been heightened or bowdlerized by the passage of time, much of the delight they remember was real—a Gallup poll taken at the time found that 90 percent of New Yorkers considered themselves happy. Few cities in the history of the world can have stood so consciously at a moment of fulfillment, looking into a future that seemed so full of reward.

"Stood": for it was ironical that a sort of stillness was part of the magic of the moment. Through the war years nothing had fundamentally changed in Manhattan—the population was more or less constant, and in many respects the 1930s had lingered on. For the first time in the city's history the place was poised rather than headlong, eyeing the future rather than plunging into it. Almost a century earlier *Harper's Bazaar* had described New York as being "never the same city for a dozen years together," and it was to become a familiar joke that Manhattan would be a great place when it was finished. But looking back now on the splendid relaxation of 1945, it seems that just for a spell the city *was* finished, *was* staying the same, as it contemplated its new status in the world and breathed the long sigh of victory. The Erie Railroad was ready to go; the Mercurys, eager for Action, were on their way to the showrooms; Mr. Robert Moses, New York City park commissioner, was contemplating his plans for a new expressway slap across the island, or alternatively a new tunnel clean underneath it; but psychologically, aesthetically too, Manhattan was experiencing a pause, in which the styles, manners and techniques of New York before the war awaited, as it were, all the new ways of living, new ways of talking and thinking, new shapes, new ideas, which were presently to fall upon the place.

For it was not long before the city was to acquire connotations less engaging. The moment of grace soon passed—it lasted no more than a few years, and by the mid-1950s was fast becoming hardly more than a regretful memory. New York was never to lose its excitement, its power to move, its limitless energy; but never again, perhaps, would it possess the particular mixture of innocence and sophistication, romance and formality, generosity and self-amazement, which seems to have characterized it in those moments of triumph.

THIS BOOK sets out to evoke the unexampled island at that unrepeatable moment of its history. It is in every way an outsider's book, about the public rather than the private city. I am not an American, so that all its descriptions have been filtered through a European sensibility. I did not myself get to Manhattan until 1953, so that everything I report is at best hearsay, at worst conjecture or extrapolation. Moreover I have confined my reportage only loosely to the year 1945, sometimes allowing it to spill over into anachronism, and have occasionally taken topographical liberties too.

So think of the experience please not as hard truth exactly, but as an exercise in affectionate and light-hearted imagination, as we dock at Pier 90 with Commodore Bissett and his 14,000 Americans, to the sound of that reverberating bass A. The hawsers are thrown to the waiting longshoremen; the gangplanks drop; and so we disembark in fancy upon the soil of Manhattan, 1945—whistling up a wing-fendered Checker cab, perhaps, or setting off on foot, under the looming shadow of the West Side Highway, along the shabby sidewalk of West 50th Street.[1]

---

[1] The *Queen Mary*, which had carried 500,000 U.S. servicemen during the war, not to mention Winston Churchill, Fred Astaire and Bing Crosby, was to sail in and out of Manhattan for another decade, before ending up as a permanently docked showboat at Long Beach, California. Commodore Bissett became an honorary Doctor of Laws, Cantab, and retired from the sea in 1947. Wilmur J. Crocker was already a millionaire, so the Sandy Hook pilots' association tells me, having resigned from the pilotage before the war and made a fortune in real estate; he had rejoined as a war service and continued to bring ships into New York until his death in the 1970s.

1

On Style

SHABBY IT MIGHT BE, but 50th Street West led one directly from Pier 90 across six undistinguished city blocks to the site that, more than any other, was the pride of Manhattan in 1945: Rockefeller Center—the state of the art, as they would later say, in enlightened urban design.

There it loomed now, resplendent beyond the Sixth Avenue which, though recently renamed Avenue of the Americas, remained a sleazy enough thoroughfare all the same: an irregular group of structures, some high, some relatively low, dominated by the jagged irregular monolith of the Radio Corporation of America building, which looked rather like a vast slab of limestone rock from which all the rest of a fissiparous precipice

15

had fallen away. Big as it was, and presided over by a financier of such inconceivable wealth that it was hard to believe him actually real and alive,[1] Rockefeller Center did not seem at all impersonal. It was asymmetrical, slightly tentative of plan really, and it had pleasant cafes in it, and flower beds, and tucked-away roof gardens for the solace of upper-floor office workers, and a sunken plaza they turned into a skating rink in winter. Easily-understandable works of modern art were dotted here and there. An observation gallery on the RCA building would give you, if the weather was too bad to see more than fifteen blocks away, a "visibility check" redeemable until 2015, when the Center's ground lease was due to expire. Even the financial origins of the complex were, so to speak, domestic—Standard Oil, the foundation of the Rockefeller wealth, had started as a producer of lamp oil, kerosene and sewing-machine lubricants. Altogether it was, though undeniably tremendous, a very welcoming, populist sort of development.[2]

---

[1] Though he certainly was—John D. Rockefeller, Jr., born 1874, did not die until 1960.

[2] As it was meant to be. Almost every facet of the street-level plan was designed to lead the public, all unwitting, gently towards its shops and restaurants. Rockefeller Center was begun during the 1930s' depression, but was making profits by 1945 (the litterateur Cyril Connolly called it "the sinister Stonehenge of economic man," but then he called Manhattan as a whole "concrete Capri").

Rockefeller Center stood in the heart of midtown Manhattan, and here as in most cities it was midtown, the area of the smartest shops, the grandest hotels, the plush offices, the theatres, the expensive apartment houses, which set the civic reputation. Manhattan's midtown occupied twenty or thirty blocks, perhaps a mile square, around the focus of, say, Fifth Avenue and 50th Street. Beyond it there stretched away wide areas of slum and dulness. To a dispassionate European observer, indeed, most of Manhattan, even parts of it much admired by New Yorkers themselves, appeared unremarkable enough—for all the impact of the skyscrapers, the average height of New York's buildings was said to be lower than the Paris average. This general physical mundanity, though, seemed no more than incidental to the predominant personality of the place, and it was here in midtown, in the Center's sunken plaza perhaps, or on a bench in the promenade between the British Empire Building and La Maison Française—it was here in the middle of things that one could best catch the public style of Manhattan (or as sociologists might prefer, the public veneer).

The Magnificent Muddle

It was above all a romantic style. Towering islanded on the edge of a continent, facing the wild ocean, Man-

17

hattan was as truly romantic a city as Venice itself, and in one way or another the look of it reflected that romance. Except for the old grid of the streets (First to Twelfth Avenues, 1st to 220th Streets), hardly anything was regular in it, whether in the detail or in the whole—there were no monumental malls, no colonnaded boulevards or pompous segmented circuses, only a bare minimum of statued squares. The civic orientation was inexact, north-south avenues running twenty-eight degrees out of true, west-east streets really running northwest to southeast, while even in midtown the wayward route of Broadway, meandering from one end of the island to the other, fatally upset the street plan and confused the anxious stranger.

Let us stand now beside the huge figure of Atlas, outside the Center's International Building, and look up and down Fifth Avenue, the grandest street in Manhattan and the nearest to a ceremonial highway—the Main Drag, "The Avenue," as old-fashioned people liked to call it, remembering the days when the palaces of millionaires had lined it, and only the *best* families had patronized its stores. It is a broad and handsome street, ornamented with elegant curly lamp-standards, two lights to a post, and ends as it happens in a formal archway (the Washington Square Arch) in a fairly formal plaza (Washington Square). It is certainly no Champs Elysées, though, its architecture mostly being a free-and-easy hodge-podge, and the imposing arch at its southern end, far from being any sacrosanct shrine to the glory of the Republic, is used as a convenient turn-around for the Fifth Avenue buses.[1]

Scarcely two buildings conform, on this splendidly individualistic street. To our left, where we can glimpse the green of Central Park beyond 59th Street, a group of famous hotels stands picturesquely cheek by jowl— the Plaza like a gigantic French chateau, the Sherry-Netherland steeple-topped, the Pierre with a mansard roof forty floors above the ground, the Savoy Plaza endearingly crowned with a pair of tall chimneys. Opposite us the twin spires of St. Patrick's Cathedral face, but certainly do not match, the varied Rockefeller elevations. To our right the tall slab of 500 Fifth Avenue, whose rooftop water tank has "500" painted largely on it, rises over the low classical mass of the New York Public Library, lion-guarded above its steps, and beyond it again there soars immensely into the sky, making the whole street vista lop-sided, the Empire State Building, the highest building on earth, with an airship mast upon its summit. In jumbled opulence the stores run away down the Avenue, this one in Gothic style, this one Renaissance. Tiffany's is a Venetian palace. Cartier's is the former residence of Morton F. Plant, the celebrated yachtsman, whose widow is still alive. Scribner's, the booksellers, is all black iron and glass. A mock-Tudor town house, with a turret and

---

[1] As it was until 1958. Now it provides shade and shelter for ice-cream vendors, and aerosol space for graffitists.

mullion windows, houses Finchley's at number 566.
Here stands an extremely churchy Episcopalian church,
here a stupendously club-like club, and far down to the
south, beyond the end of the avenue, rises the distant
raggety cluster of towers, spike-topped, pyramidical,
slim or hefty, which is the downtown financial district.

All this makes for an impression of magnificent
muddle. Like Venice, the place is all dapple. Its lights
and shades are intense, and endlessly varied—the
shadows of the skyscrapers slant-wise across the avenues,
or plunging the cross-streets into cavernous darkness,
the sudden black that New Yorkers prefer for their bars
and restaurants, the flicker of bridge girders upon passing cars, the dense patterns of fire-escape ladders, the
shifting silhouettes of park trees along sidewalks, the
tenebrous gloom, speckled and latticed with light
through the ironwork above, that lurks beneath the
tracks of the elevated railroad. On a bright summer
day, like the one we have been experiencing, the skyline
of Manhattan seems to stand against the blue like a
masonry thicket, or a huge jagged palisade; in winter,
when the tops of the skyscrapers are sometimes lost in
cloud, their bases suggest so many gigantic roots or
trunks, and the life of the city seems to proceed as
within a gargantuan forest.

"In the Air"

It was an architecture, one might say, of frozen movement. It did not look built to stand still, and artists who portrayed it in those days sometimes imagined it in violent motion, even its skyscrapers on the go, even its bridges bent with energy. Of course this was a matter of history or temperament more than of civic design, but even so architecture did have something to do with it. For one thing the shapes of mid-century, midtown Manhattan had been inescapably affected by zoning laws, first introduced in 1916. These tried to separate residential and commercial areas, grouping skyscrapers together and giving rise to the idea of Manhattan, expressed by the visionary architect Hugh Ferriss, as "a wide plain . . . from which rise, at considerable intervals, towering mountain peaks." The laws also decreed that buildings above a certain height must recede from the vertical to leave more open sky. In theory this meant that tall buildings might best be pyramidical in shape, in practice it resulted in the ziggurat form which was so characteristic of Manhattan in 1945—masonry steps wherever you looked, of different bulk and different pitch, "filling in the zoning envelope," as the architects called it, and piquantly intensifying the effect of angular disorder.

And for another thing, Manhattan in 1945 had hardly discovered the International Style of architecture, the functional, pure and box-like style which had been born in Europe earlier in the century. There were a few structures in Manhattan which seemed half-committed to the style, and one or two which had entirely succumbed, like the brand-new and very un-ornamental Museum of Modern Art; but most of the architecture which dominated midtown, and set its visual tone, was still Moderne or Art Deco, standing somewhere halfway between Beaux Arts and Bauhaus. The greatest of the interwar skyscrapers ("scrapers" as the slang had it) were buildings rich in decoration, curious devices of symbolism or pretence, quirks and allusions. They set out, as Frank Lloyd Wright re-marked, not only to amaze, but also to entertain, and they were jubilantly eclectic of style; one of the most brilliant of their designers, Raymond Hood, said of himself that he was "as much in the air about style as I am about everything else."

The predominant look of Manhattan, then, was beguilingly idiosyncratic. A building might be made of bricks of a dozen different colours, or clad in artificial textiles, or decorated with Aztec motifs, or flaunt a big glass globe on top, or sprout with sculpture and abstract images. Skyscrapers of colossal technical accomplishment incorporated decorations from Gothic or Renaissance masonry, and exhibited craftsmanship that would per-fectly have satisfied William Morris and his arts-and-crafts colleagues of the previous century. Ecclesiastical references were popular—the Paramount Building (1927) was the Cathedral of Motion Pictures, the Empire

State Building (1931) was the Cathedral of the Skies, just as the Woolworth Building (1913) had long before been called the Cathedral of Commerce; gargoyles and quaint drip-stops were not uncommon, and in the public areas of many buildings the lights were kept low and reverent. All in all it was an architecture simultaneously fanciful, swanky and strong, and as such it perfectly suited the mood of Manhattan in victory.

Most people loved the island's public style. Country innocents were dazzled by it, European sophisticates were delighted by it. New Yorkers themselves, of every class and kind, revelled in a visit to the bright lights and spectacular shapes of midtown—most of all perhaps on the day of a parade, when the beat of the drums and the blare of the trumpets, the booted, spangled, plumed and satiny paraders, the preposterously strutting drum-majorettes in their high white boots and hussar hats, gloriously complimented the resplendent buildings all around. Naturally there were dissenters. Einstein found Manhattan two-dimensional. Frank Lloyd Wright thought it now carried entertainment too far, and called it "an affected riot." Henry Miller declared it the most horrible place on earth. Edmund Wilson professed to think it no more than an unscrupulous real-estate speculation. Le Corbusier called it a catastrophe.[1]

They were however in a very small minority. Most

---

[1] But a handsome one—"a hundred times I have thought, New York is a catastrophe, and 50 times: it is a beautiful catastrophe" (*When the Cathedrals Were White*, 1947).

people loved it, and felt themselves the younger, the brighter, the more amusing for its punch and varied display—even the Museum of Modern Art, that vanguard of a more demanding modernism, so far compromised with the spirit of the town as to announce itself on its roof, for the benefit of tourists on the observation platform of the RCA building. For this was a surprisingly homely city still—in the English sense of the word, that is, meaning human and friendly of manner, if not of scale.

Midtown Manners

Manhattan is probably the most photographed town on earth, and there are pictures extant which record for us the whole of Fifth Avenue in the late 1940s, from its beginning at Washington Square to its abject conclusion, on the northern shore of the island, with a Dead End sign beside the Harlem River. The midtown scenes vividly depict the modes of Manhattan people then. They look at once jaunty and decorous. Fifth Avenue was one of the busiest streets in the world, but still its traffic seems surprisingly restrained and self-disciplined,[1]

---

[1] As late as 1964 V. S. Pritchett could still describe New York drivers, in his book *New York Proclaimed*, as "the gentlest and most mature of any great city in the world" (but I must say I think he was being kind . . .).

and pedestrians too seem to be moving about without much jostle, walking upright, arms swinging, as befits a citizenry that feeds itself well and is very conscious of its health and hygiene—some striding benevolently down the sidewalks, some, like Scott Fitzgerald's Tom Buchanan on this very Avenue, in an "alert, aggressive way, his hands held out a little from his body as if to fight off interference. . . ."[1] Hats are distinctly in fashion, tilted, often fussily flowered for women, grey trilbies almost always for men, and the gesture of holding a hat on with one hand while grasping the shopping bag with the other is among the most common of Fifth Avenue attitudes.[2] Skirts are worn discreetly below the knee, and not a pair of trousers can be seen upon a woman's legs, only well-aligned seamed stockings—"Are my seams straight?" was a familiar marital inquiry of the day. Here and there one notices a black man in a high white collar and a largely knotted tie, or a patrician figure with a derby hat and an elegantly cocked walking-stick. It is an extremely well-dressed, prosperous-looking citizenry, not in the least subdued it seems by the pressures of the metropolis; and it looks to a foreign eye

---

[1] And travelling at an average speed, so the Works Progress Administration guide to the city had estimated six years earlier, of about 300 feet per minute.

[2] At a subway station on 42nd Street, scoured as it is by ferocious ventilating winds, a notice still says HOLD YOUR HAT—an injunction interpreted by Michael Leapman (*The Companion Guide to New York*, 1981), as a general metaphorical warning about the swirl of the city waiting up above.

absolutely American—far more distinctively American, in dress, in manner, in stature, than New Yorkers would look three or four decades later.

The Avenue itself appears in these old pictures eminently refined. The Fifth Avenue Association kept a firm grip upon the protocol of the street, forbidding unsuitable businesses like gas stations, funeral parlors, dance halls or pet shops, let alone beggars or buskers; though clearly not all the people in the photographs are rich, and most of them are probably visiting from more ordinary parts of town, still they all seem to share a distinct air of privilege—the privilege of being on The Avenue at all. Above them the suggestively elegant names of stores are announced in equally carriage-trade calligraphy—Bonwit Teller, Bergdorf Goodman, Lord and Taylor, Saks; and the shoppers seem to move with a matching grace, as though they are deliberately living up to a legend.

Here a photographer takes us one Easter morning to the sidewalk outside St. Thomas's Church, at the corner of 53rd Street—what shiny Episcopalian eminence of topper and carnation buttonhole, of mink cape, white glove and veiled blossomy hat! Here we watch the small boys paddling, *almost* wetting the hems of their short trousers, in the lake at Central Park; they do it with no sense of defiance or abandon—on the contrary, they are looking almost shamefacedly over their shoulders to make sure they are not disapproved of. And how trimly, on a winter day, the young mother takes her children for a walk in the cold sunshine towards the

Metropolitan Museum—she herself in a black felt hat and a neat two-piece suit, her little boy all buttoned in a snuggly kind of ski-suit, and invisible in the depths of a low-slung luxurious perambulator, there in the heart of the metropolis, a Manhattan baby!

Such was the pictorial consensus. One photographer of the period, though, depicted Fifth Avenue differently—Andreas Feininger, who had arrived in Manhattan from Europe only in 1939, and who was obsessed with the city's irresistible momentum. Feininger's Avenue too was full of finely-dressed, bravely-striding people, and paraded by stately buses; but by dramatically foreshortening the view with long-focus lenses, he contrived to convey a much more disturbing city prospect—urgent, unrelenting, jam-packed, seething, as though the urbane ease of appearances, even then, masked more desperate realities beneath.

The Old and the New

Even in Feininger's version, the street looks clean. Mid-Manhattan was, everyone seems to agree, remarkably clean by city standards—at Rockefeller Center there were men whose only job in life it was to scrape up gobbets of discarded chewing gum. Even the honky-tonk quarter around Times Square, where the hookers flourished and the servicemen mooched around looking for

27

kicks, was surprisingly free of garbage. It was as though the stricter manners of earlier times and older cultures had not yet been eroded—as though even the roistering sailors remembered now and then the injunctions of their parents, first- or second-generation immigrants perhaps from Sweden or from Germany, about clean living and good behaviour. (It was after all milk—all those 35,000 half-pints of it—that the fighting men most wanted when they filed off the *Queen Mary*.)[1]

This was an essential part of the Manhattan style, too—not exactly the conflict, but at least the wary meeting, in this dynamic metropolis, of the old American ways and the new. Peter Conrad has pointed out (in his *Art of the City*, 1984) that one archetypal Broadway musical of the day, *On the Town*, portrayed Manhattan as a sort of country Main Street sublimated; and it was perfectly true that provincial America never felt far distant—just over the Hudson River, only a few hundred yards away, all the rest began. Manhattan cast a spell upon the whole nation, but grass-roots America, which provided a large proportion of Manhattan's residents, many of its tycoons and nearly all its visitors, fought back sturdily enough. The unmistakable slang of Manhattan, derived largely from the Yiddish out of

---

[1] Milk was the Great American Health Drink in those days, and most of the soldiers had been forbidden to drink the European varieties, on tuberculin grounds. A disembarking soldier of the 112th General Hospital Unit (so I am told by one of his comrades) drank so much that he threw up on the quay.

Europe, was overlaid by homelier Americanisms from the heartland, idioms more Norman Rockwell than Damon Runyon—"Oh boy, oh boy," "Take it easy, buddy," "Gee!," "Scram!," "Get a load of that!," "And how!," "Swell," "Step on it," "What's the big idea?," "Howzat again?"[1] Echoes of a more Anglo-Saxon America hung too around the terminology of the town. Rockefeller and his developers debated for some time before deciding not to spell it Rockefeller *Centre*, and people sometimes asked for their bill when they wanted to pay the check, went up in a lift rather than an elevator, lived in a flat or even stood in a queue.

In many ways the Manhattan newspapers were like small-town papers still. The *New York Times*, one of the chief newspapers in the English language, printed alongside its earnest summaries of world events items of local gossip which might easily have come, were it not for their degree of social pretension, from any country weekly. We read for example, as the war against Japan draws to a close, that "Mr. and Mrs. Francis Rogers will leave today for Southampton, Long Island, to spend the summer at Honeysuckle Cottage, their place in the Shinnecock Hills," or relaxing our attention for a

---

[1] For at least thirty years afterwards most of these slang terms were regarded as contemporary American idioms by the world at large, and even now elderly foreign comics trying to guy American manners will begin their soliloquies with "Say" or "Gee" (though they are likely to end them with "Have a good day," a later usage that seems to strike most outsiders as irresistibly laughable).

moment from the economic situation of western Europe, we are startled by the triple headline

MARY COTTER WED
TO NAVAL OFFICER
Bride of Lieut. James Millard
Jr. in Hartsdale Church—
Reception at Golf Club

Neighbourhood standards of propriety and fair play were still in evidence, in a public politesse that every foreign visitor wondered at, and in an institutional gentlemanliness which, however specious its intentions, at least gave an effect of concern.

Thus (or so the story goes) one day John D. Rockefeller, Jr., visiting incognito his uncompleted Center, found himself unceremoniously dismissed from the building site by a foreman. He thereupon determined to give the public a better chance to watch the progress of the work, and so there came into being an institution truly emblematic of postwar Manhattan, the Sidewalk Superintendents' Club. Originally, at Rockefeller Center, it really was a sort of club, and passers-by were given tickets of admission; later it was just a viewing platform with peepholes through which one could watch the bulldozers and the scaffolders at work (and sometimes with lower observation holes, only two or three feet above the sidewalk, for "Junior Superintendents").

Around the corner from its office, upon its former premises in Times Square, the *New York Times* maintained an illuminated sign, the Motogram, whose 15,000 electric bulbs announced the news headlines every evening. When the Motogram was switched off, after midnight, one final message was displayed, high above the pleasure-seeking crowds below: "THE NEW YORK TIMES," it courteously spelt out, "WISHES YOU GOOD NIGHT." And in the same paper's executive dining room, when they entertained guests to luncheon, the following ecumenical grace was printed with the menu:

> *O Lord, the Giver of all Good,*
> *In whose just hands are all our Times,*
> *We thank thee for our daily food,*
> *Gathered (as News) from many Climes.*
> *Bless all of us around this Board,*
> *And all beneath this ample roof;—*
> *What we find fit to print O Lord*
> *Is after all the pudding's proof.*
> *May those we welcome come again,*
> *And those who stay be glad, Amen.*[1]

---

[1] I have kept my copy from a luncheon I enjoyed at the *Times* in 1953. The grace was written by John H. Finley (1863–1940), who was briefly editor of the paper, but had been chiefly famous as an indefatigable walker of Manhattan. Always hatless, generally with a blue thistle in his lapel, he strode the entire island in a gait known as the Gandy Dance—two short steps, one long—which had been devised by railwaymen to facilitate their walks along the cross-ties. Everyone knew him, and today beside the East River there is a promenade named after him.

Personal manners were similarly considerate, by and large. Few foreigners commented then, as they would so often later, upon the rudeness of Manhattan. On the contrary, they far more often wondered at its formality. At one social level they were sometimes astonished to find small girls, brought into the apartment dining-room to say goodnight to the guests, actually *curtseying*. At another they were gratified by the shop assistant's unvarying "You're welcome," or the diligent care with which the businessman, shaking the hand of a stranger, slowly repeated his name to get it lodged in the mind—commercial acumen, but courtesy too. Punctiliously did every man remove his hat, when a woman stepped into the elevator; diffidently did the murmur come "Out, please," when somebody wanted to leave. No gentleman would allow his girlfriend to open her own car door—and no self-respecting lady would think of stirring until he had trundled around to open it for her. The conversations of well-bred New Yorkers were like alternate monologues, slowly and carefully delivered; nobody interrupted until the train of thought was pursued to its conclusion, and it was time for a reply.

Partly, one supposes, all this was a heritage of the immigrants, striving to assume American ways and master American systems. Partly it was the influence of the ruling caste of Manhattan, a powerful alliance of Anglo-Saxon and liberal Jewish whose courtly manners, often disguising notably uncourtly aspirations, seemed to most New Yorkers the criterion by which all manners should be judged—the polished behaviour of the American Gentleman, still in those days to be encountered in this city's streets, giving up his place to ladies in taxi lines, or emerging spruce and well-luncheoned from clubs.

Moralities

Nobody would pretend that Manhattan was a particularly moral, still less a puritanical town. Although it was true that burlesques and strip shows had lately been restricted, during the past four years the city's film censors had banned only twenty movies, most of them foreign, out of 5,864 submitted.[1] And when, during the war, Washington had decreed a midnight curfew everywhere in the United States, the mayor of New York declined to comply, insisting that Manhattan of all places had the right to live it up at least until one in the morning.[2]

Nevertheless religion in this city was powerful, and could be spectacularly uninhibited. Of course innumer-

---

[1] At the end of 1945, all the same, they created a rumpus by proscribing a distinguished thriller, *Scarlet Street*, directed by Fritz Lang and starring Dan Duryea and Edward G. Robinson— probably because at the end of the film a murderer was left at large in New York City.

[2] He got away with it, but in May 1945 the national curfew was lifted anyway, and from that day to this Manhattan's clubs have officially closed at 4 a.m.—at which time many unofficially open.

able churches, chapels, synagogues and missions, up and down the island, honored their various faiths with modest piety; however, many another house of worship was built for maximum effect, in the Manhattan way, and greeted the Divine in less humble style. As it happened, work was shortly to be abandoned on the Methodist Broadway Temple, inspired by the slogan "Restore the Cross to the Skyline," which was originally intended to be the tallest structure on earth.[1] But the ecumenical Riverside Church was quite lavish enough, with its thirty-story belfry tower, its seventy-one-bell carillon, its club-rooms, nurseries, theatre, gymnasium and bowling-alley, while Temple Emanu-el, on Fifth Avenue, was claimed to be the largest synagogue since Solomon's temple, and the Episcopalian Cathedral of St. John the Divine, though only half-finished, was already the largest Gothic church in the world. As for the Salvation Army, it had lately built itself a monumental Art Deco headquarters, the Centennial Memorial Temple on West 14th Street, from whose magnificent auditorium "Onward Christian Soldiers" must have sounded inspiringly indeed at the 42nd Division Armory of the New York National Guard, immediately across the way.

---

[1] Splendidly imagined in its entirety in one of Hugh Ferriss's architectural drawings, it never got further than the smallish church and two office blocks, meant to provide its financial support, which may still be seen graffiti-scrawled and mostly Spanish-speaking at Broadway and 174th Street.

Some of the city's religious moments could be wonderfully Manhattan, too. There was the Sunrise Service held on Easter Sunday in Radio City Music Hall, itself a prodigious representation of sunrise whose illuminated rays, swelling from the proscenium arch, changed color during the devotions under the direction of the theatre's light orchestrator. There were the thrice-weekly performances of sacred music on the organ of Grand Central Station, when the concourse rang to hymn and Hallelujah Chorus, and the Christian message was relayed inescapably from Oyster Bar to ticket office.[1] Or there was the annual yuletide arrival of the Salvation Army musicians in the bar of the 21 Club, the most famous of Manhattan's post-Prohibition drinking-places —a moment of richest sentimentality, by now a tradition, when the tuba players in their high-collared jerkins, the tambourine ladies in their bonnets, performed all the old Christmas favorites to the tearful and open-handed applause of the assembled merry-makers.[2]

Stars and Personalities presided over many of these celebrations—Manhattan's holy men were often very famous. The most gifted of the synagogue cantors drew huge congregations; hot-gospelling preachers of diverse

---

[1] The organist was expressly forbidden to end these occasions with the national anthem, because an inadvertent performance of it had once brought the entire movement of the station to a halt. (From *Grand Central*, by David Marshall, 1946.)

[2] It was the only music ever heard at the 21, which then as now eschewed all entertainment.

sects were great men among the blacks of Harlem. Norman Vincent Peale, pastor of the Marble Collegiate Reformed Church on Fifth Avenue at 29th Street, had given a phrase to the language as the author of the fabulously best-selling *Power of Positive Thinking*; outside his Dutch Reformed church well-heeled disciples of many denominations, from all over the United States, stood in line on the sidewalk for Sunday morning sermons.[1] Another household name was Harry Emerson Fosdick, pastor of Riverside Church, whose preaching style was said to have affected the whole tenor of American Protestant sermonizing. An essential rotund figure at any reformist rally, protest meeting or debate on human liberties, he had argued irrepressibly down the years for pacifism, birth-control and the right to drink alcohol, and was a passionate supporter of evolutionism in the Apes-v.-Angels, Darwinian-v.-Creationist debate.[2] And one of Manhattan's best-known citizens was Francis Spellman, archbishop of New York, described by *Life* that year as being "No. 2 Man among the 350m Roman Catholics of the World." Small, plump, hot-tempered and Irish, Spellman was a poet, a licensed aircraft pilot,

---

[1] The church is called "Collegiate" because in its denomination, the oldest in Manhattan, ministers are known as "colleagues." It is called "Marble" because its interior is made entirely of marble. Dr. Peale was its fortieth minister, and you can now buy his sermons on cassettes there—"Have a Terrific Time Living," or "Try Happiness, It Works."

[2] A debate which, by the time of his death in 1969, he wrongly supposed his own side to have won.

a publicity-seeker, a charmer, a theologian of reactionary tendencies, a cultivator of rich friendships, a confidant of Presidents, a public figure variously considered guileless and Machiavellian and later to be suspected of homosexual tendencies—in short, a true Manhattan celebrity.[1]

In and out of church, devoted audiences hung upon the words of such sages, but inevitably the war had brought new values to Manhattan, values racier and more distasteful to citizens of the old school (not everyone, even in the euphoria of the moment, was amused by the lieutenant waving her lace underwear at the porthole of the *Queen*—"She is not in *our* outfit," another nursing officer told the *Times* reporter severely). America's war had not been very long, and it had been fought far from Manhattan. Nevertheless the experience of it, the passage through this city of hundreds of thousands of young men on their way to and from foreign parts, had coarsened things rather, in conventional eyes, or loosened them up in others. The wolf-whistle sounded now in the streets of midtown, lean and rangy servicemen shifted their gum to the other cheek as they eyed the sidewalk broads. Manners were changing. "I was in your town last week," wrote a

---

[1] Spellman's father was still alive in 1945, and the archbishop liked to quote his paternal advice: "Son, always associate with friends smarter than yourself, and that shouldn't be hard to do." Spellman became a cardinal in 1946, supported McCarthyism in the 1950s and died somewhat discredited in 1967.

provincial correspondent to the *Daily News*, "and gave my subway seat to a lady who was going to have a baby, and some fat, lazy, slimy jerk . . . almost knocked the poor girl down making a dive for it."

Still, Manhattan had never been a very saintly place, and the out-of-towners who visited it were generally prepared for the worst. They expected urbanity, but they expected stridency too. If Rockefeller Center seemed reassuringly considerate and civilized, a few blocks away Times Square was the world's epitome of splash—in those days you did not think of Vegas, when you wanted to conjure up the images of cheerful vulgarity, but first and always of Broadway. Back to their full glory after the wartime years of dim-out, the lights of profit and of show biz flashed and flickered through the night—the dazzle of the theatres and huge picture palaces, the roof club of the Astor all ablaze, the tireless progress of the Motogram round and round—the cascading of the electric waterfall, showering pedestrians sometimes when the wind was wrong—the Camel man blowing his gigantic smoke rings—the perpetual golden showering of peanuts, the tossing heads of Budweiser horses—electric hands waving, electric feet tapping, forests of light bulbs winking, spinning, marching and pullulating.[1]

---

[1] Though Times Square was actually at its *brightest* in 1919, the last year when all its bulbs were incandescent rather than neon— their light was entirely white, which is why it was called "The Great White Way."

Around the corner, 42nd Street offered some tawdry enough establishments—peep shows, dubious cafes, shooting galleries, flea circuses, horror-movie houses and numerous unlovely examples of what the gossip columnists then called "niteries." Only particularly straight-laced Americans, however, seem to have found the Times Square quarter distasteful. Like the rest of midtown Manhattan, it had a frank and jolly air to it, and there was an impudent naïveté even to its naughtiest activities. "Hello Folks," said the lights above the burlesque houses disarmingly, in inverted commas, "Welcome One And All"—and so perhaps it felt less of a betrayal of one's poor old mother, as one went inside to inspect Tantalizing Vickie or visit the Paree Rendezvous.

But anyway, religion or no religion, Riverside Church or 42nd Street, a type of Manhattan citizen very frequently encountered was the Generally Decent Man. He was a common kind of American in those days, when inherited moralities had not yet become clouded, and the rules of the Judaeo-Christian religion were part of most people's everyday behaviour. The only official Boatman on the municipal establishment was Buck McNeil, who had been stationed for more than thirty years at Battery Park, the southernmost tip of Manhattan. He was the most famous of American life-savers, having rescued from the harbour at least a hundred people in his time. He had often been decorated, and frequently written up in the city newspapers, but seemed quite unaffected by his celebrity. If interviewers asked him what his feelings were, when he plunged yet again into the mucky water to save another life, he always answered in more or less the same way. "It's my habit," he used to say, "it's just my nature, that's all. When I sees 'em tumble in, I goes after 'em."[1]

Technology

It was almost an item of faith that any technical advance, in any field of ingenuity, found its first application in Manhattan. Technological marvels were part of the myth of the place (and it was no accident that the work of making the first nuclear bomb was code-named the Manhattan Project—the original research had been done at Columbia University on Morningside Heights). The city itself was one glorious announcement of technique, standing as it did so stupendously upon the bedrock, and extending itself every year into land-fill around its edges. Its more intrusive hillocks had nearly all been flattened, and until 1895, when the channel between the Harlem and Hudson rivers was artificially deepened, it had hardly even been an island. Many a building boldly emblemized the techniques that made it great. The Chrysler Building was ornamented

---

[1] I take his words from *Portrait of New York*, by Felix Riesenberg and Alexander Alland (1939).

not only with eagle-gargoyles like the mascots on Chrysler cars, but with friezes of semi-abstract mudguards and gigantic radiator-caps of stainless steel. The American Telephone and Telegraph building was capped with a heroic golden statue called *The Genius of the Telegraph*.[1] The International Press Building, in Rockefeller Center, was embellished all over with communicational paeans—"The Spirit of Movement Takes a Message Across the Oceans," or "Electricity Receiving Tribute from the Inventor of the Morse Code."[2] The two great railroad terminals, Grand Central and Pennsylvania Station, were universally recognized as temples to the power of steam, or at least of diesel electric (though one was modelled upon the Baths of Caracalla, and both made it quite certain that nobody but passengers ever saw a train at all).

Some of the best-known wonders of the city were ageing by now—the war had interrupted progress, and inventions of an earlier generation had been reprieved. Thus the Horn and Hardart Automat restaurants, to which every Manhattan visitor was sure to be introduced, had actually been around since 1912; but never

---

[1] It was by Evelyn Beatrice Longman, and now greets visitors like an oracle inside the lobby of the AT&T headquarters on Madison Avenue.

[2] *Viz.* Samuel F. B. Morse, who lived and died in New York City. In his lifetime he was perhaps better known as a painter and as one of the founders, in 1825, of the city's National Academy of Design, but the left hand of his statue in Central Park reposes nevertheless upon a key-tapper.

mind, it was still fun to put your nickels in the slot, open the little glass door and extract your lemon meringue pie, and the brass dolphin-head spouts through which the coffee flowed still managed to give an impression of the shape of things to come. The subway system too was past its first flush; but it was the biggest and fastest in the world, its trains traveling sometimes at seventy miles an hour, and it remained a thrill to find yourself rocketing headlong through those hellish tunnels in the direction, if you were like most out-of-towners, of God-knew-where. And curiously enough, though the just-completed George Washington Bridge, a glorious six-laned road bridge of bare steel across the Hudson, was the second longest bridge on earth, still people wondered far more at the sixty-two-year-old Brooklyn Bridge, with its ancient mesh of laced and knotted hawsers, whose engineering statistics could still make the mind reel.[1]

But there were innumerable more contemporary astonishments to assure the world that New York was indeed the City of the Future. Where else, after all, did businessmen commute to work by seaplane or by speed-

---

[1] Corbusier though was more excited by the George Washington, which he declared the most beautiful bridge in the world, and "the only seat of grace in the disordered city." Its designer, the Swiss-born O. H. Ammann (1879–1965), had already built the Triboro and several other New York bridges, and was to go on to build the Verrazano Narrows, the greatest of them all. In his old age, his widow once told me, he liked to sit in his penthouse in the Carlyle Hotel looking at them all through a telescope.

boat? Where else did security guards look through X-Ray Mirrors, or secretaries drop the morning mail down mail chutes 800 feet long, iced to prevent the letters catching fire? Where else, in 1945, could you have your photograph taken by an unmanned machine (the Photomaton), or go to a theatre on the fiftieth floor of a skyscraper (the Chanin Building), or for that matter get an electric shock just from touching a door handle, in a city so charged with energy that the very air tingled with it? At the Western Union office on Hudson Street you could send a Facsimile-gram, a telegram transmitted in your own handwriting. At Keen's Chophouse, on West 36th Street, customers could inspect stereoscopic colored pictures of the house specialities before they chose their dinner. In the RCA building a wooden Mexican nightingale, covered in silver lead, sang a recorded bird song every hour. Radio Station 627 broadcast nothing but code numbers directed to subscribers to Aircall, a radio-paging service, and when General Eisenhower gave a victory address at City Hall that summer General Electric's Noise-Meter was on hand to assess the applause as "equivalent to 3,000 peals of thunder at the same time."

A particularly Manhattan marvel was the elevator, which here reached new heights of virtuosity. It was less than a century since the first Perpendicular Railway had been seen in the city, and even in 1945 all office building elevators were worked by operators, but the elevator had long been essential to the Manhattan mystique. New York was said to possess a fifth of all the elevators in the United States, carrying 17.5 million passengers every day halfway, in aggregate, to the moon: when the operators went on strike in September 1945, the city was half-paralyzed. The Empire State high-speed elevators had lately been slowed down, from 1200 feet per minute to 1000 feet, because people sometimes felt seasick in them, but the newer RCA elevators, the fastest in the world, travelled effortlessly at two floors per second without making anyone queasy. The elevator was part of Manhattan's decor, being often elaborately panelled in rare woods or inlaid metals, and it had also irrevocably affected the external look of the city: the need for elevator banks, decreasing as the building grew taller, sometimes dictated the number of step-backs, and so the silhouette of a structure.

All this meant that Manhattan people were already accustomed to mid-twentieth-century mechanisms—a great technological gulf stood between this city and the rest of the world, or even the rest of America.[1] The underground quarters of Rockefeller Center, with their intricate networks of pedestrian ways, shopping concourses, interconnecting escalators and elevators, were a foretaste of what other cities would be like in the next

---

[1] In John Cheever's story *O City of Broken Dreams*, 1946, a character arriving in Manhattan from the Middle West did not realize that he must tell the elevator operator what floor he wanted when he first got in. "This branded him as green to all the other people in the car . . . and he blushed." When he left the elevator the operator sneered at him.

generation. The electric eye door, which was not to make life easier for Europeans for another couple of decades, was ubiquitous here. The characteristic noises of Manhattan already included the grinding night-thump of the automated garbage truck and the hum of the air conditioner.[1] There were more radio stations here than anywhere else on earth, speaking to more radio receivers per head than anywhere else. There were more telephones in New York City than in any foreign *country*, except only Great Britain. Telephone exchanges still had names and initials (PEnnsylvania for instance, or BUtterfield) but most of the telephones were by now the modern one-handed kind—no more, in Manhattan, that clutching of the trumpet to the ear!—and so enormous was the demand for them that the Bell Telephone Company installed half a million new units in the second half of 1945 alone. Radio-telephones in cars were not uncommon: the Mayor, Fiorello La Guardia, had once impulsively used his to call the Lord Mayor of London and invite him over for a visit.[2] Even the wiretap, presently to play so baleful

---

[1] Though no office building was completely air-conditioned yet, and when the Stork Club claimed in 1945 that its cooling system made use of "one hundred per cent outside fresh air," the *New Yorker* commented sourly that its customers must be liable to asphyxiation.

[2] The Lord Mayor declined, so La Guardia told John Gunther (*Inside USA*, 1946): "My dear fellow, I'm only in office for a year, don't-you-know, and I have 2,500 social engagements already."

a part in American affairs, was already familiar enough in New York, having been invented there, it was said, for police purposes in the 1890s; by 1945 official agencies, private detectives and villains of many varieties were using bugging devices all over the city.

The shops of New York were enough to make a foreign visitor dizzy with innovation. Eye-glasses for example were not just round, steel or horn-rimmed, as they were everywhere else, but came in a myriad shapes and colors. Nylon stockings, hardly more than a rumor in most of the world, were commonplace in Manhattan; the magic word "denier" was entering everyone's vocabulary—until then everyone had bought stockings by gauge—and already the silk-stocking vote was looking for a new name. Then there was the wonderful Lucite-barrelled Parker 51 fountain pen, "made to write dry with wet ink,"[1] and the Emerson self-powered pocket radio, "with no outside wires protruding from its unbreakable Tenite case," and there were deodorized sanitary towels, a consummation scarcely to be conceived in most societies, and trouser suspenders with clips instead of button-loops, and kiss-proof lipsticks, and decaffeinated coffees, and Scotch tape, and flavored adhesives for the gumming of envelopes, and floatable swimsuits enabling you to strip under water and swim

---

[1] Made in fact specifically to be filled with Parker's new fast-drying Quink, and named to commemorate the company's fifty-first anniversary in 1939.

46

in the nude, and the stereophonic Hammond Novachord keyboard, the first of all synthesizers, and health devices ranging from domestic blood-pressure machines to a thousand absolutely infallible and medically approved patent restoratives—*"Have you taken your proper dose of Amunos?"* urgently demanded the advertisements.[1]

As for the cars of Manhattan, they looked to foreigners utterly of this city; cars like no others in the world, so big, so flashy, so rich in chromium plate, so powerful but so easy-going as they waited silently for the lights on the avenues, or slid sinuously around the futuristic cloverleaf intersections on the Henry Hudson Parkway. Manhattan without cars would have seemed a contradiction in terms. As a matter of fact Manhattan people were far less interested in cars than most Americans, and the Fifth Avenue Association indeed thought them so lacking in class that they would not allow an automobile showroom on the street.[2] Nevertheless those Dodges and Buicks, those Packards and now ageing Hupmobiles, those new Studebakers that looked the

---

[1] I take most of these examples indeed from contemporary advertisements, but the trouser suspenders with clips I remember vividly because my brother Gareth came home with a pair after a wartime visit to Manhattan.

[2] Until 1968, when General Motors put up their showrooms on the site of the old Savoy Plaza Hotel. On the other hand some biologists thought the high level of carbon monoxide in the Manhattan air accounted for the lack of flies and mosquitoes, while admitting it seemed to have no effect upon the cockroaches.

47

same front and back,[1] even the box-like electric trucks left over from the 1930s, or the two-cylinder, twelve-horse-power, air-cooled Crossley convertibles, appeared absolutely native to the place—like its fauna, so to speak.

And in the middle of Manhattan there stood the ultimate monument of technological achievement, the Empire State Building, the Eighth Wonder of the World. It was less than fifteen years old, and had been put into full use only during the war (in the slump it had been dubbed the Empty State Building), but it had already attained mythical status. It was the city's crown. It was the building that King Kong had stood upon. Legends of many kinds were told of it—how Henry Ford, learning of the immense excavations required to build it, thought it might have a disastrous effect upon the rotation of the earth—how, when a B-25 bomber flew into its eightieth floor, Betty Lou Oliver a stenographer fell seventy-six floors in an elevator—how a sandwich man climbed thirty-one floors with sustenance for businessmen during the elevator strike—how when a strong wind blew the building swayed several feet in each direction.[2] Everybody went up the Empire State

---

[1] Which I first set eyes on when they were supplied to a United Nations commission of inquiry in Palestine in 1946, and which seemed to me then, as they moved in convoy around the narrow dusty lanes of the Holy Land, more or less like vehicles from Mars.

[2] Ms. Oliver survived to raise three children and keep a grocery store in Arkansas. The sandwich man was tipped $75. The building, it was determined in 1956, never sways more than $1/4$" each way, or $1/2$" in all. Mr. Ford was wrong too.

Building, every visiting film star, everybody's aunt, every serviceman on leave, every child on a school outing. The ride on the vibratory elevators, as they shot upwards in the Longest Uninterrupted Elevator Ride Above The Earth's Surface, offered one of the best-loved of all the city's varied frissons, and making a recording on the top to send home to Mom and Dad was almost a sine qua non of a visit to Manhattan. There was nothing like the Empire State Building, in all its glamor, its grandeur and its 1265 feet. Even Englishmen, in those days given to attitudes of general disdain, were impelled into admiration. "Gives quite an impression of height, doesn't it?" said one of them when asked for his reactions.[1]

Wonder City

It was a boast of Manhattan that it belonged to the people. The craft of public relations, itself a Manhattan invention, was still in its infancy, but already the institutions of the island successfully fostered this illusion. The information desk at Grand Central was briefed to deal not only with inquiries about the New York Central train timetables, or even the 1600 other railroad timetables then current in the United States, but about any

---

[1] Reported by Eleanor Early in her *New York Holiday* (1950).

matter under the sun.[1] The New York Stock Exchange already had a viewing gallery, something almost beyond the imagination of its counterparts in Europe, and the Waldorf-Astoria, at least in the popular view the fanciest of all the Manhattan hotels, offered guided tours to the public.

It was not benevolence. "Our purpose," said the stationmaster at Grand Central, asked about that information service, "is to serve the public"—but in this context as in many another, that was simply a euphemism for making money. The effect was happy all the same, and the economic self-interest of New York, which was unbridled, and had created an elite of unprecedented wealth and power, paradoxically did make the place feel the property of all its citizens. Like everyone else, New Yorkers were amazed by it, and loved to think of such a marvel as their own. "There is nothing," the waiters at the Waldorf used to tell their foreign clients, "absolutely nothing that we cannot serve you"—and they said it as though the hotel and all it stood for, all the fame, all the profit, belonged personally to them.[2]

This constant proprietorial astonishment was essential to the ambience of Manhattan then. This was the Wonder City, the Last Word on almost anything. Were

---

[1] So popular was the service that each information clerk was reckoned to answer more than 167,000 questions a year—by my calculation well over a question a minute, allowing for holidays.

[2] Alas, when they said it to me in 1953 I asked for calamari, and they didn't have any.

not the Rockefeller Center roof gardens four times the size of the Hanging Gardens of Babylon? Had not one Manhattan building after another gained the title of the highest building on earth (the Eiffel Tower being, by general consent, not so much a building, more an *object*)—after the Singer, the Metropolitan Life; after the Woolworth Building, 40 Wall Street, the Cities Service Building, the Chrysler and the matchless Empire State?[1]

Though Manhattan had been in existence for more than three hundred years, its physique was very young. You need not be an ancient, in 1945, to recall when Park Avenue was still a set of sunken railroad tracks, when the Woolworth Building went up, when the first Manhattan subway ran, or even when St. Patrick's Cathedral was dedicated (in 1879). There were plenty of people alive who had attended the opening of the Brooklyn Bridge, and remembered a Manhattan whose highest structure was the 280-foot spire of Trinity Church on Wall Street.

So even those who had lived there all their lives must have been amazed at the sheer spectacle of the

---

[1] All still standing now except the Singer Building—and even that enjoys the posthumous distinction of being the Tallest Building Ever Demolished. The Empire State was topped in 1970 by the World Trade Center towers in lower Manhattan, but in 1977 the title was snatched from New York at last by the Sears Roebuck building in Chicago (a brutal plan to add another eleven floors to the Cathedral of the Skies—"One must not be cutesy," said its putative architect—having fortunately been aborted).

contemporary city; and probably amazement was most easily stimulated at night, for then not only were those neon waterfalls gushing, those illuminated peanuts falling, those smash hits announcing themselves so dazzlingly along Broadway, but the whole center of Manhattan was a fabulous display of electric lights. Wartime restraints had been lifted.[1] Nobody had ever heard of an oil shortage. The office towers of mid-Manhattan habitually left all their lights on when the day's business was over—cliffs, ridges, humps, mountains of light, which masked the night sky altogether when the weather was clear, and whose glowing reflections hung like a canopy on the air when clouds were low. In 1945, that year of ruin, it was perhaps the most astonishing spectacle in the world. It was a fantastic declaration of wealth and waste. The "nothing-is-impossible" conviction could not have been more explicitly expressed, and there was no pathos at all to the obverse of the display, which you could see only if you trained binoculars upon some of the lower skyscraper windows—the sight of the night cleaners, in headscarves and flowered pinafores, bent over their vacuum cleaners in empty offices.

---

[1] The dim-out had been half-hearted anyway, compared with Europe's black-outs, and was introduced because it was thought that ships at sea would make easy targets for torpedoes when silhouetted against the city's glow: there had certainly been U-boats about—one landed a party of spies on Long Island.

Waste? "Why," said a down-and-out to a British visitor, "the garbage thrown away in this city every day—*every day*—would feed the whole of Europe for a week." He said it with true satisfaction, the satisfaction of accomplishment, for the gargantuan profligacy of the city was certainly part of its wonder. The unimaginably expensive apartments of Fifth Avenue, Park Avenue or Sutton Place were complacently pointed out by dwellers in walk-ups, and the most admired statistic about almost anything concerned the cost of it. Everywhere in midtown was the patina of unembarrassed wealth—in the smoke of Cuban cigars, in the hauteur of uniformed doormen, in the behemoth Cadillacs purring by, in the scalloped canopies which like wedding fitments, or arrangements for state occasions, crossed the sidewalk from the doors of any establishment aspiring to class.

And in the allure of mink. Mink had become a sort of civic substance, the subject of endless jokes but the very badge of success in the Manhattan social race. If one had to choose a single emblem to represent the wonderful opportunities of Manhattan, 1945, as most of its inhabitants probably saw them, one could do worse than choose mutation mink, which had been first produced only three years before, and was now bringing startling new colors to balls, weddings and opening nights. In 1943 2,500 mutation minks had changed hands at the New York pelt auction. In 1945 they sold 30,000—enough for four hundred coats.

Sights and Sounds Which Bring a Thrill

Planners already foresaw this city so transformed one day that Manhattan '45 would seem tame and ordinary by comparison. There were seers at large, and they imagined the whole of the East River filled in, for instance, or the whole of midtown enclosed beneath a plastic geodesic dome. They depicted huge elevated pedestrian ways, traffic in subterranean troughs, aircraft flitting here and there among the canyons, sky gardens, aerial golf courses, apartment blocks on Hudson River bridges, landing strips on the tops of skyscrapers.

For most people, though, Manhattan was quite marvellous enough already. The electric excitement of it, its emanations of intense modernity, its avid acceptance of anything new, anything extraordinary—all this, set against its titanic confusion, made them feel that just at the moment, in the second half of the 1940s, this was the best of all places to be. Never mind the crime, never mind the poverty and the ugliness which, concealed by that glittering midtown personality, was swathed across so much of the island; a postcard on sale in the Manhattan tourist shops properly spoke for nearly everyone:

> *Shining towers, in the sky*
> *The Torch of Liberty, lifted high,*
> *Blazing lights, of the Great White-way.*
> *Spelling glamor—bright as day!*
> *Flitting traffic—everywhere*
> *Bridges hanging in the air*

Tooting tugboats, never still—
Sights and sounds which bring a thrill!
That's New York, where dreams come true,
Her magic skyline welcomes you![1]

---

[1] An apostrophe written by Irwin Copeland and published by the Shining Hour Publishing Company.

2

On System

IN A GROUND-FLOOR OFFICE in City Hall, downtown, warmed by a coal fire and without a telephone in it, there sat in a condition of more or less constant gesticulation one of the most remarkable men in America: Fiorello La Guardia, the Little Flower, born in a tenement in Varick Street, not half a mile away, brought up in Arizona, trained as a lawyer, and now the ninety-ninth mayor of the City of New York.

This was no mere honorific, and certainly no sinecure. There was no city in the world whose mayor was more powerful a public figure. The job was, as it happened, traditionally a dead end—few mayors had gone on to be governors or senators, and none had ever become President. But it was quite big enough in itself, and it kept its incumbent always in the headlines. Whether a mayor was elected to office corruptly or honestly—whether the machine he headed was genuinely democratic, or was a mere front of vested interests or opportunism—whether he distributed his patronage justly among the citizens, or gave everything to henchmen—whether he was a crook or a statesman, an idealist or a charlatan, the mayor of New York was *ex officio* a star. His name was usually known far outside New York, often far outside the United States. He lived in the fine old Gracie Mansion overlooking the East River, and had his office in the very same marble-faced building, opposite the Woolworth skyscraper on lower Broadway, that had won an international competition for City Hall in 1803 (it was then considered to stand so absolutely at the northern limit of urban expansion that they did not bother to put marble over the brownstone back, on the grounds that hardly anybody would see it).[1] He moved about his city in ostentatious flummery, attended by aides and motorcycle policemen like a head of state, and was habitually to be seen in ceremonial parades waving at the crowds from the backs of Cadillac convertibles. He consorted with presidents, kings, prime ministers

---

[1] In 1954 the back was marbled like the rest. Very proper too, thought the architectural critic Ada Louise Huxtable (*Classic New York*, 1964), City Hall being "a symbol of taste, excellence, and quality not always matched by the policies inside."

and all manner of celebrities. And when he retired, two small carriage lamps affixed to the front door of his private house showed that its inhabitant had once been, wonderful to recall, Mayor of New York City.

Hizzonor

Between the wars the tone of New York had been set by one of the more dubiously engaging of its chief executives, James J. Walker—Gentleman Jim, Beau James. An Irishman through and through, he had depended upon a loyal web of Irish ward captains and agents, and was a true link with Manhattan's free-booting, entertaining, crooked and cozily Irish-dominated political past. Dapper and elegant, Walker had a lovely singing voice, wrote the lyrics of the song "Will You Love Me in December as You Do in May?," married a chorus girl, drove a smashing Duesenberg and once said he would rather be a lamppost in New York than mayor of Chicago. When he fell from power in 1932, having been revealed guilty if not exactly of corruption in himself, at least of allowing corruption in others, many citizens found it easy to forgive him. He had resigned in a haze of scandal, and sailed away to live it up in Europe, but had come home to New York in 1940, and foxy as ever with his stick and his light grey fedora, was unashamedly enjoying himself still.[1]

He was Old New York. La Guardia, the man who had replaced him, was decidedly New. Though the Little Flower had been in office since 1934, having been twice re-elected, he was essentially a modern man, perfectly suited to see political Manhattan through its transition from reckless provincialism to the authority of world supremacy. Not that he was colorless—few mayors of New York had ever been that. On the contrary, in his own way he was just as striking as Gentleman Jim. He was the son of an Italian father and a Jewish mother. He married first a Catholic, then a Lutheran, and was himself a lifelong Episcopalian. He was short—5′2″— swarthy and thick-set, like a wrestler, and talked in an unexpectedly high-pitched voice. He wore very wide Stetson hats (hence his nickname "The Hat") and very long coats, and he seemed to be all a-fizzle with energy, hot temper, resolution and reformist zeal: a *New Yorker* cartoon of the day showed City Hall itself shaken to its foundations, as by an earthquake, when his Honor arrived in the morning, only settling down to its old composure when he drove away at night. He was a very clever man, an excellent linguist, and widely experienced, having served as a clerk with the U.S. foreign service, as an

---

[1] He died in 1946. He spent his last years at 120 East End Avenue, but when I inquired there recently after Jimmy Walker the doorman said: "He doesn't work here any more."

Army pilot in the First World War (another of his nick-names was "The Major"), as a congressman in Washington and as the national director of civil defense during the War: but he had directed the greater part of his energies to the running of New York.

"Nobody wants me but the people," La Guardia said, and this was possibly true, for politically he was a kind of hybrid. A Republican, he was a New Dealer too, had always been on good terms with Democratic administrations in Washington, and since 1936 had held office with the support of the American Labor Party— "I've never belonged to any political party," he said once, "for more than 15 minutes." Also he was an inflexible fighter of municipal corruption. He had broken the grip of the New York Democratic machine, Tammany Hall, and he it was whose policies had scoured Manhattan of its most blatant gangsters, banned its criminally-organized gambling, cleaned up its theatre, cleared its streets of pedlars and pushcarts, and exposed Gentleman Jim's appalling laxities. Myth said that when La Guardia was originally sworn in as mayor, on December 31, 1933, the very first thing he did was to pick up the telephone and order the arrest of "Lucky Luciano," the most powerful mobster in the city.

"La Guardia's main weakness," remarked the *Daily News* sarcastically of his attack on fruit machines and gaming houses, "has been a Puritan streak . . . gambling was a cancer eating out the slimy soul of American manhood, or something like that. . . ." But the people loved him all the same, forgave his occasional prudishness, admired his long fight against, as he put it, "political riff-raff, chisellers, racketeers, tinhorns." They liked his volatile style and his diligent brand of showmanship: when *The Firefighter* was christened, at La Guardia's suggestion, by the fireman's daughter with the best school record that year, the Mayor himself decreed her dress for the occasion—a white dirndl gown with a red fire cape. They were amused by his frankness: "When I make a mistake," he said in a celebrated *bon mot*, "it's a beaut."[1] They enjoyed his fondness for popular music, especially when he conducted the combined Police and Sanitation Department bands at their annual Carnegie Hall concerts ("Does Hizzonor want any special arrangements, extra lighting perhaps?" "Hell no, just treat me like Toscanini").

Since 1942 the people had also listened in their millions to his Sunday morning broadcast talks direct from City Hall, which covered every subject under the sun, from how to help children with their homework to the best ways of eating fish—"Ladies, I want to ask you a little favor. I want you please to wear your rubbers when you go out in this weather. If you don't wear your rubbers you may slip and hurt yourself . . . Now another word about fish." In 1945 there was a strike of newspaper truck drivers, and the children of Manhattan were denied their comics—in those days absolutely essential

---

[1] He said it supposedly of his decision to rename Sixth Avenue the Avenue of the Americas—a change ignored to this day by most New Yorkers.

to the fulfillment of young Americans. La Guardia read them instead over the radio—"Gather around children, and I will tell you about Dick Tracy—Aah, what do we have here? The gardener! Stabbed! . . . *but Dick Tracy is on the trail. . . .*"

In fact New Yorkers would probably remember La Guardia more vividly for his reading of the comics that year than for anything else, but he was really far more than a mere populist He was, as he said himself, "an inconsiderate, arbitrary, authoritarian, difficult, complicated, intolerant and somewhat theatrical person," but history would recognize him as one of the most original of all American civic administrators. Now he was sixty-two, and had been mayor of New York longer than any-one else. He was suffering from a terminal cancer, and was tired, and thinner than he used to be. His old fury had abated. His ball-like figure no longer bounced with quite the same effervescence from meeting to meeting, appearance to appearance. In the summer of 1945 La Guardia was in the last months of his revolutionary mayorality, and slackening. It was intermission time at City Hall.

Master Builder and Mr. New York

The administration of New York City was extremely elaborate—like the government of one of the lesser republics. Within it all the five boroughs of the city were equal, maintaining their own borough presidents, district attorneys, school boards, planning boards, courts and commissioners, but the headquarters of the whole structure were in Manhattan, which in political parlance was actually called New York County. After so many years of La Guardia's attentions, it was generally claimed to be the best and most honest city administration in America, and it employed many interesting men. At one extreme there was Buck McNeill the modest life-saver of Battery Park, or Mr. Anthony Mazza the solitary city game warden, uniformed in ranger hat and Sam Browne belt, whose job it was to see that wild animals were not cooked at restaurants and protected creatures not sold at pet shops. At another extreme the city employed some of the most prominent of all New Yorkers. Let us introduce ourselves to two of these, one a Jewish intellectual with a visionary view of urban change and an exquisitely urbane literary style, the other a self-educated Irish businessman with a taste for protocol and a gift for pageantry.

Robert Moses was officially the park commissioner, but he was much more than that. He was the autocratic grand panjandrum of planning, conservation, reclamation and demolition. More than any other man, he set the physical tone of Manhattan in those years. "We aim," he once said, "to rebuild New York, saving what is durable, what is salvable, and what is genuinely historical, and substituting progress for obsolescence." A towering patrician figure, standing head and shoulders above his patron La Guardia, he came from a long-settled and well-to-do German Jewish family, was educated at Yale, Oxford and Columbia, and accepted no salary from the city, only lavish expenses.

Moses began the pursuit of his aims uncontroversially, energetically building new parks and improving old ones. By the late 1940s, though, he was organizing the progress of New York with god-like grandeur—the Master Builder, dreaming of huge expressways, tunnels and towers, obliterating neighbourhoods, moving people here and there, and making of Manhattan the first true auto-city, where the private car had priority over public transport. His attitudes were lordly. Never having learnt to drive a car himself, he maintained a staff of twenty-four-hour chauffeurs, and had offices all over the city, some of them with private dining rooms and chefs. He was accused of callousness, megalomania and Philistinism, but "if the end doesn't justify the means," he used to say, "what does?" His vision of New York's future was cerebral and lofty—a city better organized, better planned, more efficient, more exciting.

He achieved it all by mandarin will-power, having little time for the usual bureaucratic processes ("Nothing I have ever done has been tinged with loyalty"), and still less for public critics ("Those who can, build, those who can't, criticize"). He sneered at architectural humanists like Lewis Mumford or Frank Lloyd Wright. He was a power in his own right, virtually autonomous within the administration, and he once held twelve city, state and federal jobs all at the same time. If he was no Gentleman Jim, he was certainly an impressive figure to find, a figure far beyond the calibre of most city administrations, in the once blowsy, frivolous, boozy and corrupt corridors of New York City Hall. La Guardia called him "His Grace": he called La Guardia "Rigoletto."[1]

Moses would have been anathema to Manhattan politicians of the old school. Grover Whalen, on the other hand, would have fitted easily enough into most New York administrations. Since by 1945 he was essentially a *visual* functionary, we will consider him not in the principle, so to speak, but in the practice. There he emerges now, out of the terminal buildings at LaGuardia Airport in Queens, striding to the edge of the tarmac where the silver DC 3 of Pan American Airways has just this minute landed. He is surrounded by aides and officials, mostly much shorter than he is, and attended by a police chief, a military officer or two, the airport administrator, three or four photographers and, lined up to the right, the New York Police Department, more probably than the Sanitation Department, band. He

---

[1] Moses died in 1981, aged ninety-two, having served five mayors. He held his last office until 1968—nobody, of any political party, had dared to get rid of him—but his final years were saddened by financial scandals involving some of his associates (though never Moses himself), by the failure of the 1964 World's Fair, which he master-minded, and by a general shift in the philosophies of urban planning. I still admire him, though, if only because of his taste for the terrific and his elegant prose.

has come to meet a president, or a monarch, or a well-known Arctic explorer, or the recently returned commanding general in Japan, and he does it with swagger; for Grover Whalen long ago found his vocation and his celebrity as the city's Honorary Official Greeter.

Could anyone do it better? He is part diplomat, part actor, part speechmaster. Tall and bulky, he wears a Homburg hat and a pin-striped suit, and in his lapel there is a large buttonhole alleged by legend to be an invariable camellia, but probably just a chrysanthemum really. The visiting fireman (as they used to call such visitors then) descends from his aircraft to a flash of photographers' bulbs, and beams as celebrities will vaguely towards Manhattan. Whalen, detaching himself from his acolytes and underlings, steps forward, removes his hat, and in a loud rich voice perceptibly tinged with brogue welcomes the visitor, on behalf of Mayor La Guardia, to the City of New York. The band plays lustily. The officials are all smiles. The visitor is almost certainly charmed. Off they go, laughing and chatting, past the gaping passengers in the terminal, out to the big black limousines awaiting them in the forecourt, and away over the bridge to Manhattan.

Whalen had come to civic ceremony via, or in parallel with, a business career (with the Wanamaker department store, with Coty's cosmetics, with Schenley's distilleries) and less glamorous municipal functions (police commissioner, commissioner of plant and structures). He had achieved a great popular success as president of the New York World's Fair of 1939, the most ambitious ever mounted.[1] By 1945 he liked to call himself "Mr. New York," having been welcoming the city's official visitors since the 1920s. He had stage-managed the colossal reception given to Lindbergh after his Atlantic flight in 1927, and by now there was hardly a bigwig in the world who had not, at one time or another, felt the hearty grip of his handshake. Although there had been ticker-tape parades in Manhattan at least since 1910, it was Whalen who had made the shredding of telephone directories, the showering of tape and miscellaneous wastepaper an essential part of every welcoming parade, and had made the ticker-tape parade itself, indeed, synonymous with Manhattan. He had founded a tradition.

Grover Whalen was immensely pleased with himself, but that was only an asset in an Official Greeter of the City of New York—a functionary who, like the greeters of oriental kingdoms long before, relied upon a stylized bonhomie. Being naturally a jolly and gregarious man, Whalen performed to perfection. As those limousines sweep away towards City Hall or Gracie

---

[1] One of the fair's themes had been "Building the World of Tomorrow." When it was ended by America's entry into the war, a well-known double-talk performer named Dave Driscoll commented: "Here was the pledge of peace which might well have been the fiederness, bedistran and goodle of this great expedition. Now that pledge is forgotten. Sleedment, twaint and broint furbish the doldrums all over the world. Alas!"

Mansion, we see the visiting grandee, deep in the plush back of the grandest Cadillac of all, smiling happily, if sometimes uncomprehendingly, at what we must assume to be one of Grover's Irish jokes.

The Sense of Order

Visitors to Manhattan were always surprised by the clouds of white steam which issued from manhole covers and hatches in the city streets, in veiled and shifting contrast to the rectilinear buildings all around. Actually these emissions came from cracks in the hot-water system, carried in 180 miles of underground piping, by which many of the buildings were heated; but to the imaginative they seemed to suggest some hidden power, some underlying System out of sight, by which the great metropolis was coordinated. Would, the Mayor might say, that it had been! Moses called the governance of New York impossible, and in the past it had probably been one of the very worst-run cities in the world—"Go Fight City Hall" had long been a despairing Manhattan *cri-de-coeur*. At our particular moment of its history, nevertheless, most strangers in Manhattan, though they may have been misled by the efficacy of those water pipes, found the city well-ordered enough.

There was for a start something sensible about the shape of it, compact, graspable, with the chimneys of

its power stations smoking busily here and there around
its perimeters, and the generally logical pattern of its
thoroughfares, avenues running north and south, with
blocks at twenty to the mile, streets crossing them east
and west. Mathematical formulae, so strangers were in-
structed, supplied keys to every locality. At the docks
you could subtract 40 from the number of the pier, and
find the number of the nearest street. To find the nearest
street if you had only an avenue address, you dropped
the last digit of the building's number, divided it by
two and added specified numerals—for 500 Fifth Avenue, for instance (the building that emblazoned its
number on its water tank) you added 18 to 25 and discovered that your destination stood near the corner of
43rd Street. The streets were mostly one-way in 1945,
but the avenues were all two-way, making it much easier
for dowagers to go shopping in their chauffeur-driven
limousines.

It was an unusually organic kind of city. Its sewage
mostly went into its surrounding waters, to be swept
away by the tides. Its garbage mostly went to make
landfill. Its corpses were nearly all removed from the
island—only one or two of the old downtown churches
still accepted burials in private vaults. Its indigent old
and its incurably sick were housed on an offshore island,
Welfare Island, in the middle of the East River. The
daily migration of its commuters, in and out, in and
out, over the bridges, on the ferries, through the sub-
aqueous tunnels, was like a great tidal movement, and
the ships that were docked all around the shore, fitted

so neatly into its multitudinous piers, made the whole island seem God-made, rather than man-developed, for its own particular functions.

Also devoted though it was to individual enterprise, more than most cities Manhattan had a sense of corporate purpose. In recent years it had even tinkered with socialism of a kind—the lowercase, New Deal kind. Public housing had appeared here and there, and the municipality had begun a form of social insurance for its own employees—the thin end of the wedge, conservatives thought. City planning had advanced since the first zoning laws: Moses presided over a planning commission, and a private organization called the Regional Plan lobbied zealously for regulated control and development. The whole of the port was run by an official body, the Port of New York Authority, the subways and buses belonged to the city and the water supply too was municipally run. La Guardia's New York was highly regarded by liberals of the time. Its old vain-glory of power, said the Federal Writers' Project book *New York Panorama* (1938), had "given way a little to the order of a genuine and mature society."

Three peoples in particular maintained this order: Irishmen, Jews, Italians. The faces of these peoples, the stance of them, the manner of talk, perhaps the manner of thinking, made the official manner of Manhattan unmistakable. Its vain-glory might have weakened in the adversity of the 1930s, but there remained something distinctly theatrical to it, streaked even in these last months of La Guardia with a touch of the raffish.

New York's Finest

The police, the most generally visible officials, sustained the impression with flair. Though there were many policemen of German, Polish and Italian stock, and even a few blacks, they were popularly supposed to be all Irish, and looked it—when Whalen passed by in his blue shirt and buttonhole, they saluted him as one of themselves. They were older, on the average, than their successors in later years, and they were of an especial build, unlike other men, unlike other Irishmen even; rather like very powerful gnomes, stout and broad-shouldered, with paunches that looked to be all muscle, and jowly humorous faces. Their thick serge double-breasted uniforms had collars buttoned up to the neck, and they wore black cross-belts, and large badges on their chests, and floppy black caps with even larger badges, and they were altogether inimitable. Nobody stood like the Manhattan cop, nobody walked like he did, nobody could twirl a nightstick quite so meaningfully, or patrol a sidewalk with quite the same motion of mingled roll, strut and heavy shamble. Perhaps he, rather than Grover Whalen, was the real Mr. New York. Certainly for all the venal scandals which periodically tainted his profession, he had long since been honored with the sobriquet "New York's Finest."

There were 20,000 policemen in the New York precincts in 1945. At their head stood Lewis J. Valentine, the longest-serving police commissioner ever—he was appointed by La Guardia in 1934, having started his career as a policeman on the beat in 1903.[1] He was a famous disciplinarian, grim-faced and blunt-spoken (when he spoke at all), but even his unbending supervision had not eliminated all corruption from the force. Many an officer still got his regular pay-off from gamblers or racketeers, or was rewarded for his blind eye with a drink behind the bar. This did not greatly shock the general public. It was all in the family, so to speak. You knew where you stood with a cop in those days, knew he would scratch your back if you scratched his, knew that if he took the law into his own hands it was generally in the cause of rough and instant justice. Even the traffic police were not too unpopular, if only because they seldom tried very hard to enforce the traffic laws— La Guardia had said that he preferred reckless drivers to kill themselves off. The Police Athletic League, acronymically known as PAL, had been set up specifically to foster good relations with young New Yorkers: it had its own radio program, and in 1945 arranged for 181,000 children to go to major baseball games, and for 50,000 more to take boat trips up the Hudson River.

Policing in 1945 was a relatively primitive pursuit, even in New York. Officers still paid for their own equipment, shoes and weapons, and some of the precinct

---

[1] He ended it by going to Tokyo, at the bequest of General MacArthur, to reorganize the police, fire and prison services of Japan, and died in the odor of integrity in 1946.

houses were preposterously antiquated—the East 35th Street house, for example, its walls covered all over with the ancient and obscene scrawlings of prisoners, was still lit by gas. Valentine's own downtown headquarters building was a gloomy neo-Baroque fortress, built in 1909, and almost the only modern installations of Law and Order were the houses of detention—the men's within the Art Deco building dreadfully called the Tombs, the women's in another Moderniste structure, on Greenwich Avenue, which echoed with the eldritch shrieks of inmates conversing with friends (and sometimes enemies) on the sidewalks below.[1] In the whole of Manhattan only four police cars and one motorcycle were equipped with two-way radios; the others had to send their messages from fixed transmitters around the city. Yet it was generally conceded that the New York force was as efficient as any in the world, and its prestige, like its morale, was high. As the writer Mary Field Parton had put it, a New York policeman should be "young and strong, tall, of good figure, lynx-eyed, sharp-eared; firm but courteous; brave as a lion but without a roar"—criteria not altogether unworthily represented

---

[1] After a nasty riot in the Tombs in 1974 the men's prison was removed to another offshore island, Riker's, while the nuisance of those screamed discourses is said to have been a principal reason for the demolition, in 1974, of the Women's House of Detention. In 1973 New York Police Headquarters also moved, into a much less forbidding building with a plaza.

73

by Mick the cop on the beat, portly, stertorous, whiskey on his breath, a ten-dollar bill in his back pocket, but still offering to the world at large some fairly genial approximation of security.[1]

To the Fires

But even the police got out of the way when, with a howl of sirens and a thrashing of 240-horsepower motors, the American La France V-12 fire engines of the New York Fire Department came sweeping into an avenue. This was a truly spectacular force. Everywhere in America fire brigades meant more than they did elsewhere, based as they often were, like lifeboats in Britain, upon communal voluntary effort. In New York, though they had long since become professional, they had an extra meaning still: partly because Manhattan had been repeatedly ravaged by fire, and was terribly vulnerable to

---

[1] Ms. Parton was writing in her book *Metropolis; A Study of New York* (1939), and added that New York policemen must not know fear—"they must enter dives and places where criminals congregate." The statistics soon worsened. Within twenty years the number of murders had more than quadrupled, and there were nearly seven times as many rapes. By then the police were often less amiably regarded, besides looking a different and less reassuring shape.

it, but partly because this city, with its immensely long straight avenues, its right-angled cross-streets and its towers all about, provided an incomparable stage for the theatre of the firefighter's art. Even in this exciting place nothing was more stirring than the charge of the fire engines through midtown on their way to a calamity. The firemen were still pulling on their jerkins, still settling their helmets on their heads, when the first of the great machines came howling and clanging out of 47th Street, say, into the line of the Fifth Avenue traffic. The cars and buses shied abruptly to the kerb as the great red thing flung itself amongst them, and screeched away down the Avenue; but before anybody had quite recovered his nerve, and just as the first bus was venturing back on its route, with a howl in a different key, a clanging of different bells, out there hurtled a second American La France—and a third behind it—and a fire chief's car, howling too—and weaving and streaking through the shuddering traffic, screaming all the way, magnificently the men of Engine Company 44 disappeared past the Empire State building, until all you could see of them were their blurs of violent red zigzagging towards Washington Square.

The fire commissioner of New York was another Irishman, Patrick Walsh, who talked in a broad brogue and looks out at us from contemporary photographs twinkling agreeably beneath bushy eyebrows and wearing an old-fashioned fireman's cap, white, high-brimmed, and with a shiny black peak. His force was described in a contemporary publicity handout as "the foremost fire fighting service in the civilized world," and it was inescapable in Manhattan. In peacetime London you might not see a fire engine go by in a month, or even a year: here seldom a day passed without one of those glorious performances. There were said to be 50,000 fires in a New York year, and 93 percent of them were extinguished within the area involved when the engines arrived. Engine houses were very numerous, and often handsome. One looked like an Italian palazzo, another like a small French chateau, and a third, on Great Jones Street, rather like a presidential mansion somewhere, while the quaint little wooden home of the *Firefighter*, Marine Company No. 1 on the waterfront down at the Battery, was among the most familiar of all Manhattan landmarks.[1] The fire houses were also popular Manhattan institutions, where carol singers never failed to call, children were sure to be lifted into drivers' seats, and Ladies' Circles were given guided tours after lunchtime lectures by fire chiefs. In poor neighbourhoods especially, where fires were horribly common, the firemen were local heroes—not corruptible, like the policemen, and generally blind to wealth, age or race.[2] In the

---

[1] As it still is, though it seems to shrink generation by generation as the skyscrapers behind it grow more enormous. *The Firefighter* is still fire-fighting, too.

[2] The only allegations I have found against Manhattan firemen are that (a) if expelled from the force they sometimes resorted to revengeful arson, and (b) they were afraid of rats.

past decade seventy-three of them had lost their lives in the course of duty: each death was marked by a ritual ringing of firebells, in groups of five, all over the city.

New Yorkers loved to watch the fires. La Guardia seldom missed a big one, and when that bomber hit the eightieth floor of the Empire State Building, bursting into flames, he climbed up there from the sixtieth floor to see the action. Dr. Ernest Stillman, a physician, had a private alarm system installed at his house on East 75th Street, so that he could be on the spot to give unpaid medical help, and the photographer who called himself Weegee (and whom we shall meet again) recorded a multitude of conflagrations. Some of his images are unforgettable. Such kindness amidst the filth and heat! Such trust! Patiently the fireman waits as an old man in a burning tenement struggles into his trousers. Tenderly an arm is placed around, not a terrified girl or a screaming housewife, but a bald-headed man in a business suit, still bewildered from the ladder. Pale and drawn the young firemen watch while the priest, woken from his bed, performs the last rites over the canvas-wrapped figures on the sidewalk. Weegee's most famous fire photograph shows a blaze at a fast-food factory, the hoses gushing, the firemen swarming on the escapes, the ladders straining high. Steam and smoke are everywhere. SIMPLY ADD BOILING WATER, says a large advertisement halfway up the building; but in the glare of the arc lights, the din of the engines, the hiss of the hoses, nobody is laughing.

Getting Educated

Politically the city had been numbed or pacified by the war and its prosperity. The passionately radical views of the Depression years, so often expressed then in protest and demonstration, were out of fashion now. Socially too, among most kinds of Manhattan residents, family life was still secure, and juvenile deliquency was not one of the city's worst problems: it merited a report in the *Times*, that summer of 1945, when a thirteen-year-old boy was found in a doorway on East 83rd Street "suffering from alcoholism and marijuana." The great immigrant groups of Manhattan—the Irish, the Italians, the Jews, the blacks—were all in their several ways bound to the ideal of family responsibility. Most of them also believed strongly in the advantages of education, and their children were taught that the one sure way of getting rich was to get educated first.

So Manhattan was a quite particularly educational kind of place—not at all a place for idle minds and idle hands. If we are to believe memories of forty years on, its public school system was generally decorous and diligent. Classes might be overcrowded, methods might be over-rigid, but the old *mores* of the American schoolroom, it seems, still held sway in this cosmopolitan metropolis, and the teacher was as respected a figure on Eighth Avenue as she was on Main Street. Besides, the aims of the system were perfectly clear, and generally accepted: not just to teach the children to be literate, numerate, artistic and good at sports, but to make proper Americans of them. Manhattan itself was one great instrument of this intent, but the public schools were its concentration, the place where children of all races, languages and faiths were taught to salute the flag each morning and say a prayer to the American God.

Few resented this. It was the natural thing. It was what parents wanted. It was what you came to America for. There was no self-consciousness about it. Black children generally went to school with black children, as was the way of the world. Yellow went with yellow. Some schools were overwhelmingly Italian, or Hungarian, or Ukrainian. Some were entirely Jewish, and said their prayers to a *Jewish*-American God (and there were three hundred private schools, too, some as they used to say "progressive," some just damned expensive). But the underlying meaning of Manhattan primary education was the harmonization of many different racial stocks into all-Americanism.

The history of the Manhattan public schools had been anything but placid, and had been embroiled indeed, since the very beginning of free education, in fearful entanglements of method and ideology. Before the war there had been school disputes which threatened not just the school system itself, but the whole administrative order of Manhattan. It was one of La Guardia's best achievements—he loved children—that he had calmed these disorders; his regime, says a historian of the system, had "finally conquered its traditional problems."[1]

But of course all ambitious families wanted college education for their children. They were in the right city for that, too—Manhattan was thick with colleges. New York University had an enrollment of 40,000, more than Harvard, Princeton, Yale, Oxford and Cambridge all put together, and two famous institutions catered especially for the poor student: the municipal City College, in Harlem, gave free residential courses to a student body mostly Jewish; the privately-endowed Cooper Union, off Union Square downtown, gave free day (or more often night) classes to students of all ages. Even in 1945, when the immigrant urge to knowledge and improvement was waning rather, these two places exuded an astonishing sense of application. Many of their students came from homes where a book was seldom read (Jimmy Walker, when elected to the mayoralty, boasted to a reporter that he had probably not read fifteen books in his whole life—and he was a law graduate of NYU!). None of them were there to while away a year or two, acquire the social graces, or just do what their fathers had done before them. The students were demanding and so were the teachers: amid the high romance of Manhattan, its merriment, its squalor, its extravagance and its greed, City College and Cooper Union seemed

---

[1] Diane Ravitch, *The Great School Wars* (1974)—but the book goes on, unfortunately, to tell of the difficulties that tormented the Manhattan public schools in subsequent decades.

to blaze away there with a steady and relentless flame, like burners cutting a way through debris.[1]

Presiding as it were over the whole vast educational edifice—over the technical colleges and the music colleges and the medical colleges and the New School for Social Research and the theological seminaries and the hundreds of grade schools—over them all towered Columbia University in northern Manhattan, one of America's oldest and most distinguished universities. It was almost like a town of its own, in its straggle of buildings above the Hudson River, and its tradition of splendid intellectualism had been raised to even higher pitch by the arrival, before and during the war, of many dazzling European scholars. Its chief was Dr. Nicholas Murray Butler, and he was the star of Manhattan's academic stars. Everyone knew of Dr. Butler, who was always in the papers, who had been president of Columbia for forty years, who appeared at functions or addressed public discussions every other day, who had written the inscription on the Gold Medal of Honor presented to General Eisenhower that summer, and who represented for aspiring Manhattan parents the very pinnacle and epitome of culture. As W. Parker Chase had said in his book *Wonder City* as long before as 1932, Nicholas Murray Butler was "about as nearly a human dynamo as this nation of ours has ever produced."

---

[1] They burn still. By 1985 City College had produced seven Nobel Prize winners, more than any other public institution; three of them were from the same class, of 1937.

See him standing there now, so solemn, so imposing. It does not surprise us in the least to know that he holds thirty-seven honorary degrees, that he has been decorated by fifteen governments, that he is a member of twenty clubs. He has won the Nobel Peace Prize, of course. He has been a confidant of many Presidents. He is a director of the New York Life Insurance Company. He is a pillar of the Republican party. He is like a permanency of the city, having lived in the University's presidential house ever since it was built in 1912, and though he is losing his sight now and is at last beginning to seem an old man, still his opinions are listened to with awestruck respect throughout the world. He is the living ideal of what a man can achieve, in 1945, in Manhattan, if he is properly educated.[1]

The Taste for Anarchy

Manhattan was reasonably safe. In most parts of the city people could move about, even at night, without worry. Drugs were only for the sophisticated rich, the truly down-and-out or the jazz musicians—certainly not for the children of the respectable middle-classes. Even

---

[1] When he died in 1947, aged eighty-five, Herbert Hoover said: "It is a pity that men of his quality could not last longer." Hoover was seventy-three then, and lasted until he was ninety.

graffiti writing was kept in check, both qualitatively and quantitatively—this is an authentic example of the period: NUTS TO ALL THE BOYS ON SECOND AVENUE—EXCEPT BETWEEN 68TH AND 69TH STREETS.[1]

Though one cannot perhaps altogether trust the statistics, the Manhattan crime figures for 1945 do not look too terrible. There were 184 murders or non-negligent manslaughters, 286 rapes, 649 robberies and 609 drug offences; but only five people, it was reported, were charged with accepting bribes, only four with bribery, and only one with embezzlement (while not a soul was accused of treason or poisoning a horse, though both categories of crime were available in the charge-sheets). This compared favorably enough with other American cities—you were three times as likely to be murdered if you lived in one of the big cities of the South—and in the New York papers "mugging" still got inverted commas. Looking back upon those times in later years, Manhattan citizens were often to remember them as halcyon years of perfect honesty and public responsibility.

But as a song popular at the time had it, it ain't

---

[1] Recorded by the broadcaster Alistair Cooke in the course of a spirited retort to J. B. Priestley, the English novelist, who had called New York "Babylon piled on Imperial Rome." In 1945 few New Yorkers knew the word graffito: they seldom know its singular form even now, but think its plural indigenous to Manhattan.

necessarily so. For all those comforting statistics, and despite all the efforts of New York's Finest, Manhattan had a natural taste for anarchy. There were dangerous parts of the city even then—of course there were: one would be foolish to venture lightly into Morningside Park, to the west of Harlem, or wander heedlessly through the dilapidated quarter of the West Side known as Hell's Kitchen, where a multi-racial population of drunks, drug addicts, layabouts and minor crooks haunted the intersections. Prostitution was everywhere: its queen, the celebrated Polly Adler, was a public figure —her bordello was repeatedly raided, her telephone was tapped, but she labored on regardless.[1] Benzedrine, hashish, cocaine, opium, circulated much more easily than the bourgeoisie realized. The armored cars so often to be seen depositing wages or collecting takings were formidable reminders that this was a tough town. Europe had nothing like them—with their heavily-riveted armoured-plating, their protrusions like machine-gun turrets on the roof, their racks of rifles, sawn-off shotguns and gas guns, they had been developed directly from military vehicles of the First World War.

And beneath the surface, out of sight of ordinary citizens, the powerful forces of organized crime were by no means extinct. In the 1920s and early 1930s they had

---

[1] She wrote a best-selling book, too, called *A House Is Not a Home*, and when she died in Hollywood in 1962 the hospital thoughtfully registered her occupation as "author."

been brazenly ubiquitous, which is why those armored cars had been devised. The bosses of Murder Inc. had been grandees of the city, and local gangs had proliferated—the Irish West Side Dusters, the Jewish Lefty Loveys and Gyp the Bloods, the Italian Dago Franks. Numbers games and protection rackets of every kind had operated with impunity. During the single decade of the 1930s there had been more than 150 gang murders in New York.

Since then a state crime commission had been scouring the underworld, and in theory the worst was over—since 1940 there had been only twenty-three killings, six of them in 1945. In fact many of the old villainies lingered on, more diffusely perhaps, but scarcely less ubiquitously. The conquering heroes of the *Queen Mary* hardly thought first of crime and corruption as they set foot upon the soil of home, but in fact they were stepping instantly into the thick of it, for the rackets of the Manhattan waterfront were rampant. The midtown Hudson River piers, which included the wharves of some of the fanciest Atlantic shipping lines, and were just down the road from Rockefeller Center, were controlled by four union leaders, every one of them a violent criminal. At Pier 90 itself, where the *Queen* docked, the hiring foreman had lately been murdered; his successor was a Mr. McKay, who was on parole from a sentence of seven to fifteen years in the penitentiary. Pilferage, loan-sharking, extortion, assault were commonplaces of the quays, and the fiscal affairs of the longshoremen's union were almost inextricably shady. The financial secretary of Local 866, interrogated later by another commission, admitted that he kept no books of any kind, either of receipts or expenditures. "As a matter of fact, Mr. Spencer, to be brutally frank about it, what you did with that money of the union . . . was to put it in your own pocket, isn't that right?" Charles B. Spencer: "That's right."[1]

But that was nothing. Imbedded deeper still within the fabric of Manhattan remained the Mafia—and not always obscured by the fabric, either, for the leaders of its five New York families were sometimes to be seen in full display, attended by underlings, fawned on by waiters in well-known city restaurants.[2] The Mafia malevolently influenced Manhattan activities as varied as drug smuggling, trucking, prostitution, garbage disposal and labor union elections, besides underwriting every kind of extortion scheme, great and small. It had lately won favors in Washington, rumor said, by enlisting the support of confreres in Palermo for the Allied invasion of Sicily—it was allegedly for this unexpected war work that "Lucky" Luciano himself (real name Salvatore Lucania) was shortly to be released from Sing Sing,

---

[1] An exchange recorded, like all this mayhem, in the proceedings of the Waterfront Commission of New York Harbor, 1960.

[2] In one of them, Umberto's Clam House on Mulberry Street, Joseph "Crazy Joe" Gallo was to be gunned down in 1972; outside another, Sparks on East 46th Street, "Big Paul" Castellano was murdered in 1985.

where he was serving a sentence of thirty to fifty years for compulsory prostitution.[1]

And as we now know, it was in Manhattan that "The Commission," the Mafia's shadowy governing body of organized crime throughout America, met to determine its policies and issue its often murderous orders. It had been started in 1931, just three years before La Guardia's arrival in office, and had easily survived all commissions, revelations and reforms since then.[2]

Postscript

So even The Major, even the magisterial Moses, even Police Chief Valentine, even the disciplines of war and the precepts of family loyalty could not really order Manhattan. Those spouting plumes of steam were less images of latent system, perhaps, than of the irrepressible opportunism of the place, which boiled and bubbled under everything. Hardly had the troops come home and the war ended than La Guardia, declining to run

---

[1] He was a criminal all his life—"I never was a crumb, and if I had to be a crumb I'd rather be dead"—and when he died of a heart attack in Naples in 1962, aged sixty-five, he was about to be re-arrested on narcotics charges.

[2] A fact revealed only in 1985, when some of its chieftains came at last to trial.

for a further term, handed over his office to a successor more of the Jimmy Walker school, William O'Dwyer, a former policeman, who was presently exposed like so many of his predecessors as a consort of crooks and a manipulator of public funds.[1] All the same, the city had been shaken to its foundations, and permanently altered, by the Little Flower's mercurial passage through its affairs. When he left City Hall for the last time another *New Yorker* cartoon depicted a citizen contemplating a portrait of his successor. "Will he be a *quiet* Mayor?" the man is somewhat wistfully asking.[2]

---

[1] He left New York to become United States ambassador to Mexico, a move described by Wallace S. Sayre and Herbert Kaufman, in *Governing New York City* (1960), as "no less a grim necessity than a welcome opportunity."

[2] La Guardia, who unlike so many of his peers and contemporaries has never been debunked, did not long survive his retirement. After what Moses was to call an "unfortunate period of random scribbling, potboiling and ill-prepared, raucous radio exhortations," he died in September 1947, aged sixty-seven. His entire estate consisted of a mortgaged house in the Bronx and $8000 in war bonds: at the news of his going the New York Fire Department, whose epic displays he had so often hastened to witness, sounded the traditional five-bell alarm, four times, early in the morning.

3

On Race

IF YOU WHIZZED to the eightieth floor of the Empire State—changed elevators—sped to the eighty-sixth floor—changed again—rocketed to the observatory at the very top of the mooring mast, 1250 feet above sea level, and looked around you, your view would extend, so the publicity pamphlets said, into five states and up to eighty miles out to sea. More to our point, you would very easily see the entire island of Manhattan, and you would recognize how small and uncharacteristic a part of it was midtown, whose style we earlier considered. There was a similar cluster of skyscrapers in the financial quarter, near the island's southern tip. There was the huge greenish, or perhaps brownish, expanse of Central

Park which occupied 150 city blocks in the very heart of the island. But for the rest, seen from that majestic eyrie, Manhattan seemed to have no particular style at all. Even at the foot of the great skyscraper—within its shadow, if you were up there sufficiently early in the morning—the streets of the West Side, running away to the dock piers of the Hudson River, were all too ordinary: blocks of dull shops and unnoticeable apartments, a factory here and there, demolition lots and car parks. Further afield whole slabs of the city, in all directions, looked not exactly blighted perhaps, but distinctly dingy.

Out there were the neighbourhoods, the multitudinous separate communities, almost separate townships, which gave a deeper reality to the myth of Manhattan. The proud and crested skyscraper city, with its magnificent avenues, was supported by innumerable meaner districts, interspersed through the municipal grid, whittling away at it sometimes, or altogether separate on its flanks. Few of them were very old. Until the 1850s, nothing much had been developed north of 42nd Street, but the neighbourhoods had extended so fast—rich people and poor leapfrogging each other as first one district, then another, advanced into fashion or fell into disrepute—they had expanded so explosively that by now the entire island, to its very last river inlet, was filled with masonry.

The real significance of the neighbourhoods however was not social, but ethnic, for many of them were quarters in the old European sense, where minorities of different races lived together in enclave.[1] In the previous century James Bryce had called New York "a European city, but of no particular country," and even in 1945 Manhattan was in many ways a very un-American place—much the most foreign city in the United States. Washington, D.C., was only now, after the heady traumas of war and victory, really beginning to interest itself in foreign affairs, and remained in essence a Southern town; Los Angeles, San Francisco and Miami were hardly international cities in those days; it was above all through New York that America looked out to the wider world, and received its multitudinous influences. Probably half Manhattan's residents were either foreign-born, or were the children of foreign-born parents; about a fifth were black; thousands of citizens thought of themselves still as Irish, or Italian, or Polish, or Jewish.

The accepted ethnic system of the time was that of the Melting Pot, which presupposed that immigrants came to America in order to become only and entirely Americans. New York, the chief port of entry, had always been considered symbolic of this process—where else could the Statue of Liberty stand?—but the pace of immigration had dramatically slackened since the last

---

[1] Though the word "ethnic" had not yet entered the Manhattan vernacular, and only in 1945, the *Oxford English Dictionary* tells me, did it first appear in print as a noun.

great wave, before the First World War. Since the 1920s a quota system had restricted the inflow by nationality. Orientals in particular were all but banned, and except for refugees from Nazi oppression, including many eminent artists and intellectuals, there had lately been few immigrants from Europe. The notorious immigration center at Ellis Island, just to the north of the Statue of Liberty, was almost out of commission, being used only for the screening of political defectors and seamen who had jumped ship.

So the city stood, in this as in so much else, at a moment of pause. The Melting Pot was off the boil and Manhattan's attitude to the older societies of Europe remained ambiguous. To be foreign still had a certain cachet. Gentlemen's clubs of Manhattan were modelled slavishly on English models; it was a poor maitre d' who could not present at least the picturesque echo of a French accent;[1] the New York Philharmonic, the oldest symphony orchestra in the United States, had never yet had an American-born conductor;[2] Olga the Bearded Lady, a well-known fairground performer of the city, found it necessary to her art to introduce herself in one context or another as the daughter of a Hungarian general, the half sister of a French duke, and a

---

[1] Old New York Joke: "I'll have a demitasse, please." "Gimme the same, and a coffee too."

[2] The first was Leonard Bernstein, appointed in 1958.

native variously of Paris, Moscow, Shanghai and Potsdam.[1] On the other hand the war had been a powerful incentive to patriotism, and there were deeply-rooted xenophobic factions in Manhattan—anti-British, anti-Russian, anti-Arab or just anti-foreign in general. The thousands of settlers who had arrived thirty or forty years before had settled deeper into Americanness, and produced children less alien still, and New York probably felt less like a city of immigrants than it ever had before: the color-coded tiles in some of the subways, introduced in the early 1930s for the benefit of illiterate newcomers, were more or less forgotten.[2]

Anyway, many of those urban splodges out there were inhabited by communities no means entirely assimilated into the All-American Way. Let us return to street level, by the Longest Uninterrupted Elevator Ride Above The Earth's Surface (some mineshaft drops were longer), and take a closer look at three of the most resilient Manhattan minorities.

---

[1] She was really Miss Jane Barnell from North Carolina, born of a Russian-Jewish father and an Irish-Indian mother, and she is described in a classic of Manhattan, Joseph Mitchell's *McSorley's Wonderful Saloon* (1943).

[2] They were revived, in a different form, to help the immigrants of the 1980s.

The Blacks

Up in the north, between say 110th and 170th Streets,—up there beyond the Park lay Harlem. People still alive remembered when it had been a bourgeois white district, and it was hardly more than thirty years since a correspondent to the *Times* had asked querulously: "Can they do nothing to put a restriction on the invasion of the Negro into Harlem? . . . They are coming closer all the time." Even now there were many long-established Italians in Harlem, and an increasing number of Puerto Ricans in what was becoming known as Spanish Harlem, in the east, and there was a community of Finns, and a sprinkling of Chinese: but to everybody in Manhattan then Harlem meant Black (or rather Negro, "black" being considered derogatory by blacks and whites alike).

Geographically it was indeterminate, almost as much an abstraction as a locality. Architecturally it was generally unenticing. Much of it was slum—the worst and most congested in Manhattan. It had no skyscrapers, and even its most important thoroughfares, Seventh Avenue, Lenox Avenue and 125th Street, look in contemporary photographs about like commercial streets in one of the lesser midwestern manufacturing towns. Socially, or artistically, it was at that moment balanced between a brilliant recent past and an uncertain immediate future. The twenties in Harlem had been climactic times, when the American black culture had first found a coherent voice, and had attracted to this capital of negritude talented and ambitious blacks from all over the world. The Tree of Hope which grew in the middle of Seventh Avenue, at 131st Street, and which was a gathering-place for actors, artists and musicians, had acquired a symbolic meaning for black people everywhere.[1] Harlem then had been one of the most truly creative places on earth, and what was called the Harlem Renaissance was remembered with regretful pride.

For by now the great days were over. Both the status and the attitude of black Americans had shifted since then, and the Depression had fallen catastrophically upon Harlem. There had been an immense influx of black people into New York from the segregated South, but though they were certainly better off here they still found themselves treated generally as inferiors, usefully fulfilling inferior jobs—forty years before every porter at Grand Central had been a white man, now all but one were black.[2] They were seldom trusted with responsibilities. There were very few black bus drivers, elevator operators or apartment block porters, relatively few black policemen and no black firemen at all, and in

---

[1] By 1945 exhaust fumes had sadly withered it; a replacement was given by Bill "Bojangles" Robinson the dancer, but it died too, and today there is only a decorative steel sculpture to mark the spot.

[2] The exception was Mr. Milton Newman, a Jew, who had been working there since 1900.

the whole of Manhattan, 1945, only 819 dwellings were owned by black citizens. Harlem had lost much of its shine. There had been ugly riots in 1935 and in 1943, crime was worsening and the district had been declared off-limits to white servicemen. White people still owned nearly all the property up there, ran nearly all the businesses; there were strong undercurrents of resentment.

Nevertheless Harlem still had allure. The one thing that black people were universally recognized as being good at was enjoyment—it was an old joke that the Jews owned Manhattan, the Irish ran it and the black people enjoyed it—and it was just for enjoyment that nine out of ten of Harlem's visitors found their way up to those shabby but celebrated streets. "Take the A Train," ran the refrain of Duke Ellington's theme song, and it meant that when you wanted a good time you took the express subway from midtown up to 125th Street.[1]

It was still an excitement, for an out-of-towner especially. You climbed those subway steps, hardly fifteen minutes from Rockefeller Center, and instantly everyone around you was black! It was like another world; but to the surprise of many tourists, in some ways it was a world much like one's own. Not all Harlemites, it turned out, were rioters, slum folk or

---

[1] The song was by Billy ("Swee' Pea") Strayhorn, 1915–1967, himself a Harlem resident, who was inspired to write it by the opening of the Sixth Avenue Independent Subway in 1940.

trumpeters! Most of Harlem was certainly drab and poverty-stricken, but by no means all. There were well-dressed men about, and women of elegance, and businessmen not at all unlike, were it not for their color, the scurrying middle-rank executives of midtown. There were even quite likely to be, if you strolled up to Van Cortlandt Park on a summer afternoon, courtly West Indians playing cricket. Here were the Harlem River Houses, a much-admired and beautifully-maintained public housing scheme, and here was the excellent Red Rooster restaurant, and here on Seventh Avenue was the Hotel Theresa, not a bad hotel at all, thirteen stories high and steam-heated throughout.[1]

Then book-browsers of any color would feel themselves at home at Lew Michaux's, which was not only a powerhouse of black thought in New York City, but every aficionado's idea of a proper bookshop. It was a marvellously jumbled place, with books by every black author, biographies of every black celebrity and black newspapers from all over—the Chicago *Defender*, the New York *Age*, the Pittsburgh *Courier*, the *Afro-American*—LYNCH TERROR HITS N.C. TOWN, PROBE ATHENS, ALA., RIOT. . . . There was an

---

[1] It was white-owned and had admitted black guests only since 1940, but had become much the smartest black hotel in America, and went on to achieve particular fame by housing Fidel Castro during his visit to the United Nations in 1960 (he had quarrelled with the management of the downtown Hotel Shelburne). It is now an office block.

art gallery for black sculptors and painters, sidewalk debates proliferated outside, and in the middle of it all, as likely as not passionately arguing politics with a group of friends, enemies or total strangers, was Michaux himself, the best-known arguer in Harlem.[1]

Places of worship reassuringly abounded. Some were sufficiently exotic, it is true: the Metaphysical Church of the Divine Investigations, the synagogue of the Royal Order of Ethiopian Hebrews, the walk-up premises of down-to-earth pastors like the Rev. G. I. Morrell— "Funerals and Marriages Promptly Attended to on Short Notice"—or the headquarters of controversial prophets like Father Divine, who was regarded by his followers as Dean of the Universe.[2] Others though were orthodox, well-endowed and famous by any standards, like the very consequential St. Philip's Protestant Episcopal Church, or the Abyssinian Baptist Church, whose congregations even Norman Vincent Peale might envy.

Good Lord, did black people really occupy these fine houses—these villas of Sugar Hill, high on the Harlem

---

[1] Who died in 1976, by which time his store had been torn down to make way for the Harlem State Office Building.

[2] The Harlem Jews, Falashas who claim descent from Solomon or the Queen of Sheba, flourish still. Father Divine, né George Baker of Savannah, Georgia, attracted the loyalty of many black people by helping them in business, and was the chief of an immensely rich cult when he died in 1965 in his ninetieth year. I fear that Mr. Morrell's own obsequies may also by now have been attended to.

Ridge, which looked just made for nannies, nursery schools and the walking of pedigree dogs—these handsome townhouses of 138th and 139th Streets, with their suavely decorated doorways, their scrubbed front steps, their alleyways through to the servant quarters behind? Could there really be Negroes living in such style, such particularly brand-new Cadillacs at their gates, such comfortable and civilized sitting rooms to be glimpsed behind their silken drapes? Was that swish tennis club, the Metropolitan, really for *blacks*?

There could. It was. Harlem's pretensions, like its ambitions, were sometimes extreme—the local swells, one black observer wrote, loved to "cavort and disport themselves in what is called the best Ofay manner."[1] Socially aspiring blacks still sometimes "passed," as the term was, for whites. Besides, some people of great importance lived in this remarkable ghetto (as they already called it). There was Adam Clayton Powell, Jr., for instance, who had succeeded his equally famous father as pastor of the Abyssinian Church. Six feet tall, athletic and wonderfully compelling of presence, he loved cars, wine and night life, married first a showgirl, then a swing pianist, and was already using his pulpit as a rostrum of black emancipation. He was not only a local hero as a champion of all things black, but a national

---

[1] Ofay being the black word for posh white attitudes, especially when adopted by black people. Its etymology is debated, but my own theory is that it is a corruption of *au fait*.

figure as New York's first black congressman.[1] There were young writers like James Baldwin, growing up in Harlem then, and old ones like Langston Hughes famous and revered. There was the distinguished lawyer Thurgood Marshall, and the eminent sociologist W. E. B. Du Bois.[2] The great black sportsmen of the day were grandees of Sugar Hill, from Jack Johnson the first black heavyweight champion of the world to Joe Louis the latest. The diminutive Father Divine was an international celebrity. And most thrillingly of all, of course, for any ordinary visitor to Harlem, one might see in the street, if not too early in the morning, or supping at the Red Rooster if late enough in the afternoon, one of the supreme black performers who still lived up here—Duke Ellington, Ella Fitzgerald, Count Basie, Billie Holiday, "Bojangles" Robinson or Cab Calloway, the aristocrats of Harlem, whose names were known almost everywhere on earth.

Perhaps it was true that the genius for entertainment—self-entertainment included—was Harlem's governing energy. Black nationalism was already fierce

---

[1] He was expelled from Congress in 1967, on charges of financial impropriety, but his Harlem supporters promptly re-elected him anyway, and though he was defeated in 1970 he remained the charismatic pastor of his church until his death in 1972.

[2] Whose courses presently diverged: Marshall became the first black member of the United States Supreme Court, Du Bois became a Communist, emigrated to Ghana and renounced his U.S. citizenship.

there, but Black Power had not yet emerged, and despite the poverty the social atmosphere was merry. Many Harlemites had come quite recently from much simpler places, and there was a tradition still of home-grown performance. A continuing custom was the rent party: anyone at all might open the doors of an apartment to the public, charge a small entrance fee, offer some home-made gin and stage a kind of domestic cabaret within, perfomed sometimes by celebrated artists of the neigh-hourhood, sometimes just by members of the family, and often by the customers themselves. Spontaneous folk music was alive in Harlem, and the stranger wan-dering the streets might find himself caught up in the sudden rhythm of a beaten garbage-can lid, or the half-dance of a couple of black boys strolling the sidewalk in front, or the exuberant if tinny rattle of a piano from some tenement. Harlem street life was vivid, for all the shabbiness of its setting. Harlem talk was swinging, hep talk, much copied by young whites, but really evolved as a semi-secret code for insiders, like thieves' English.[1] Harlem fashions found their epitome in the zoot suit, with widely padded shoulders and a long, long jacket, worn (it might be) with a white doeskin waistcoat, very pointed suede shoes, a pork-pie hat and a long watch

---

[1] For instance, Cab Calloway revealed in his *Hepster's Dictionary*, to blow your wig meant to be extremely excited, to kill me meant to give me a good time, a dracula was anything in a class by itself, and your main on the hitch was your husband. The argot was called "jive," a word only later applied to a manner of dancing.

chain looping from the trouser belt almost to the ankles. Harlem music lay, *au fond*, behind all the popular styles of the day: behind swing, and bebop, and boogie, behind the trucking—behind the jitterbugging, that very celebration of young America, with which Captain Astheimer's girls greeted the men on the *Queen Mary* home from the foreign wars.[1]

To go to the roots of this music, to discover the sources of all these high spirits, was most strangers' chief purpose in going up to Harlem. The practice was nothing new—was indeed well past its prime. In the 1920s and 1930s, when all the great jazz musicians still played in the Harlem clubs and dance halls, it was very much the thing to go "slumming it" in Harlem—take the A train up to Jungle Row, as they used to say, for yardbirds and strings (fried chicken and spaghetti, that was) and an evening at the Savoy Ballroom, the Apollo Theater, Small's Paradise or the Cotton Club. All the young Manhattan socialites did it, taking with them fashionable foreign guests, and so did many young artists and intellectuals—in those days, it was said, only Paris could match Harlem for the excitement of new ideas and unconventional ways. So smart had it then

---

[1] Not everyone approved of these influences. "The Lindy Hop," wrote O. O. McIntyre, (*The Big Town*, 1935) "is a barbaric throwback to the dervishes of the jungle. . . . In Harlem, it is said, many of the better exponents are those hopped up by smoking the reefer, a drug that has the wild stimulation of hasheesh."

become, in fact, that presently the famous performers had mostly been lured away to play at clubs and restaurants elsewhere: bop music, which had been evolved at Minton's Playhouse in Harlem, was now best heard in establishments far downtown where black audiences were not welcomed. Even some of the Harlem clubs themselves—notably the world-famous Cotton Club—had migrated to white man's country, and by the late 1940s only a few of the celebrated Harlem establishments were still open around 125th Street. They had been, in their way, part of the Harlem Renaissance, and history had thinned them down.

But there were still enough to lead a constant stream of hedonists to Harlem, and they still conducted their business with an incomparable panache, laced with bitter irony—they were nearly all owned by white entrepreneurs, and even up there in Harlem some of them admitted only white clients. It was still a great experience, to enter one of these legendary pleasure-places after dark (in mufti, of course, if you hadn't yet been demobilized). The sense of *gleam*—black skins set against white collars, or rhinestoned silver lamé! The controlled raucousness of the music! The forbidden smell of marijuana! The particular oblique resonance of the voices! The endless innovations of dance step and syncopation! The frisson, if you chose the right club, of spending an evening jammed tight on a dance floor, hugger-mugger or even cheek-by-cheek with people of another color! Such were the allurements shared among all white ranks and classes, of a night out in Harlem, on the flip side of the Big Apple.[1]

The people of Harlem bore with it. They did not, as a whole, bear much malice towards whitey as an individual, and if we are to believe the black writer Claude Brown, were mostly rather afraid of him.[2] Tourists were as safe in Harlem as they were anywhere in New York. But then the district was, by its own standards, rather muted in 1945. Broken windows and abandoned houses were a reminder of the wartime riots, but the charismatic racial leaders of the next generation, the Black Power men, had not yet declared themselves. It was a waiting time. Duke Ellington called contemporary Harlem "an illusion." The poet Arna Bontemps, who had lived there in its fascinating heyday of the 1920s, returned on a visit twenty years later and found it, he said, "another place."[3]

---

[1] A nickname first given to New York, as it happens, by black jazz musicians (though Mr. Calloway, I see, defines "apple" in jive talk just as Harlem itself). One theory is that since they used to call a gig an "apple," a gig in New York was a "big apple"; others say it simply signified sweet pleasure, good taste, and temptation.

[2] We probably can, for Mr. Brown was himself a graduate of several Harlem street gangs. He made the observation in *The New York Spy* (1967).

[3] Today it is another place again, far more battered, dangerous and depressed than it was in 1945. Its population has halved since then, and all over the place there are derelict or burnt-out houses damaged in disturbances or, more often, just abandoned by their

The Jews

Although in fact many of the Harlemites, including some of the most famous, were West Indian by origin, most people thought of blacks as native Americans. When they thought of immigrants in 1945, they were likely to think first of the East European Jews.

There had been Jews in Manhattan since the seventeenth century, and by 1945 25 percent of New Yorkers were Jews, compared with a proportion of less than 2 percent in the country as whole, and less than 0.02 percent in rural America. Jews dominated the New York theatre, were influential in the law, in journalism and in finance, and provided half the public-school teachers. There was a large Jewish intelligentsia, a large Jewish proletariat too, and over the generations a stratum of German Jews, in particular, had risen to great power and prosperity in the island, honoring for the most part a liberally reformed kind of Judaism, and known to themselves genially as Our Crowd.

---

landlords. Puerto Ricans have moved into East Harlem and Upper Harlem. Most of the old establishments have gone, but Small's Paradise has survived and the Apollo has recently re-opened with much publicity, while others periodically attempt revivals. A tentative process of gentrification has begun, they say, and some white families are moving back to Harlem; few indeed, however, at least as I write, are the tourists brave enough to take the A train up there now. The chief literary source for our own visit has been Jervis Anderson's *This Was Harlem* (1981), but the more callow white responses were mine, in the 1950s.

In common parlance, though, a Jewish immigrant was a descendant, or a survivor, of the mighty influx of Jews who had arrived from eastern Europe around the turn of the twentieth century, escaping the tyranny of the czars. They had mostly been poor, illiterate and rigidly orthodox of faith, and they had settled in successive waves in the area of lower Manhattan, near the East River, which was known colloquially and approximately as the Lower East Side. There they had established a community richly fertile, lusty, earthy, tough, ambitious, pathetic, gifted and sometimes outrageous, with its own lively Yiddish vernacular. Many of them had long since graduated to more comfortable districts uptown, notably on the west side of Central Park, where they had been reinforced by refugees from Nazi Germany and had established a thriving middle-class Jewish society, richly intellectual, with its homes on Central Park West, West End Avenue and along Riverside Drive, and its own adopted restaurants, like the Eclair and the Tip Toe Inn, which were transformed from all-American eating-houses into substitute *Konditorei*. Nevertheless in the late 1940s some 200,000 Jews were still living within the two square miles of the Lower East Side. Many of them were still as staunchly and introspectively Jewish as ever,[1] and this corner of

---

[1] Harry Golden, in his book *Only in America* (1958), reports the following Lower East Side dialogue: "What's all the fuss about?" "There's a wild lion broke loose!" *"Is that good for the Jews or bad for the Jews?"*

lower Manhattan retained a powerful ghetto-like sensation, architecturally at least far more confining than Harlem's.

There was hardly a decent house in it, by contemporary American standards. It consisted mostly of jerry-built tenements, some surviving from the days when an opportunist landlord could put his tenants into any kind of hovel—buildings where, as the saying was, "The sun is ashamed to shine": teeming, scrambled, piled buildings of brownstone, laced with iron fire escapes, hung about with washing. They were built very close to one another, giving the whole quarter a darkened, almost medieval look, and the synagogues which often stood among them, loomed over by their dingy bulk, made one think of onion domes in slatternly Russian towns.

The shopping streets were still very, very Jewish. The once-famous handcarts, so absolutely emblematic of the original immigrants, had been banned from the streets now, but the Hester Street market on a Sunday afternoon, when the pavements were thick with stalls, cardboard boxes, dresses hanging from poles, awnings, resolutely jostling shoppers and indefatigably shouting salesmen, was still the nearest thing in Manhattan to an Eastern bazaar—a place where everything was marked down, or sale price, or remaindered, or new shipment, or final stock, where a really determined housewife could buy all she needed for her home and family in a single street, on a single afternoon, and where rich *émigrés* from the quarter would often reappear in their smart limousines to do an economical week's shopping.[1]

In many streets Yiddish signs were at least as common as English, and everything in sight was pungently Jewish. The people themselves looked extremely Jewish, whether they be old Russian couples, in long coats, walking silently hand in hand along the sidewalk as though they had never left Kiev, or absolutely New York housewives out for business, purses at the ready, shiny black shopping bags over their arms, faces set in formidable resolve not to buy anything at more than a knock-down price. Shop after shop in Essex Street was full of Jewish religious objects: bar mitzvah sets, talaisem, yarmulkes, Torah mantles, mezuzahs. Elsewhere all was Jewish food, bagels and lox, fresh-grated horseradish, fruit-flavored cheeses, onion rolls, pickles on big outdoor stands. There were famous knish shops like Yonah Schimmel's, which had been putting potatoes into pastry crusts since 1910, and bakeries like Gertel's, fragrant with challahs, corn ryes, pumpernickels and chocolate icings, and candy stores like Julius the Candy King, in the Essex Street market, which fulfilled for the abstemious some of the functions of a saloon. There were hosts of movie houses, the Ruby, the Windsor, the Palestine, the Florence—Lower East Siders had loved the movies from the start—and plenty

---

[1] Most of Hester Street has since been demolished, but the nearby Orchard Street market still offers, on Sunday afternoons, much the same vital scenes.

of bookshops, and well-known restaurants like the Garden Cafeteria, where the Yiddish press people liked to go, or Ratner's famous for its cheese blintzes, or the Lupowitz where Rumanian gypsies played the violin. On Rivington Street was the venerable Schapiro's Winery, the only winery in Manhattan, where in premises marvellously musty wines pressed from upstate Concord grapes were put into bottles under scrupulous kosher supervision—rich sweet wines most of them, made famous beyond the bounds of the ghetto by Schapiro's advertising slogan "Wines You Can Almost Cut With a Knife."[1]

Up the now shabby and colorless Second Avenue, between East Houston and 14th Street, was the area they used to call the Jewish Rialto, in its time an astonishing forcing-house of talent. Here one could still see the façades, if nothing more, of the theatres that once represented a climax of Yiddish culture: the Orpheum, the Public Theatre, the Yiddish Arts, home of the most famous of all Yiddish repertory companies, the Grand, where the almost supernally handsome Jacob B. Adler had filled every seat at the turn of the century. One or two limply survived as live theatres, the rest had been turned into shops or movie houses, and among them there still precariously functioned the Cafe Royal, on

---

[1] Many of these establishments still thrive. Julius the Candy King is on the same market stand, Unit Stand 100, that it has occupied since 1900, and Schapiro's, still a family concern, now also offers kosher wines from France, and kosher sangria.

the corner of 12th Street. This was a place of nostalgic pilgrimage for many Jews because it had been in the twenties and thirties a resort of Parisian allure, a meeting-place for artists and writers of all kinds, where sightseers came to stare at the great men sitting over their coffees, and ideas had been thrown about from table to table all day long for a couple of generations.

There survived, too, some of the institutions founded long before to help ease the Jews into American life—the settlement houses which had provided every assimilative tool from literary class to shower-bath, the famous Yiddish newspaper, the *Jewish Daily Forward* (*Forverts* in Yiddish), which had been since 1897 at once the mouthpiece and the guardian of the immigrants. Lordly in its eleven-story tower, a skyscraper by the standards of the neighbourhood, in 1945 the *Forward* was still producing each morning, if in rather smaller press-runs than it used to, its inimitable mixture of material: stern, sometimes hectoring editorials, news columns enlivened by dispatches from correspondents in Paris, London, Palestine, and above all a celebrated advice feature, "Bintel Brief" ("Bundle of Letters"), which was halfway between an agony column and a social advisory service. Here are two characteristic "Bintel Brief" inquiries of the period, addressed as was the custom to the Worthy Editor, with the answers they received:

A woman signing herself "The Worried Mother" reports that her younger son, aged nine, has become a vegetarian. Her doctor has told her to have patience, but "there is no end to it—he refuses to eat anything that was once alive.

Worthy Editor, advise me what to do. I'm afraid my son
will grow up to be sickly."
Answer "The mother is advised to find out where her son
got the idea to be a vegetarian, and then, with the help of
a specialist, she might be able to bring him to eating meat
and fish . . . A good doctor would know how to treat her
9-year-old vegetarian."

"Your reader H.Z." says that her 8-year-old orphaned
nephew is being looked after by a Gentile family, and they
are reluctant to give him up. "They are fine people, but
I don't want my brother's child to remain with the Gen-
tiles . . . Help me to save this Jewish child from getting
estranged."
Answer "Knock on many doors, write letters to special
offices. H.Z. is given hope that somehow she will be able to
get the child away from the Gentile family."

But Worried Mother and H.Z. were like voices
calling from long before. As the East Side Jews dispersed
across the city, and lost something of their intense
communal loyalty, so by 1945 they were looking back
to the years before the war with a detectable nostalgia,
balancing what they had gained with what they had
irretrievably forfeited. In America these were, in many
ways, golden times for Jewry. The horror of Nazi Germany had put anti-Semitism to shame: if there were
private clubs or social neighborhoods still reluctant to
accept Jews, publicly hardly anybody now would have
the bad taste to be openly anti-Semitic. Jewish jokes
were out of favor, and even in literature characters with
Jewish names were sometimes found, when reprints

were called for, to have been unexpectedly Gentilized. On this continent, at least, it seemed for the moment that God had answered the prayer of the Yiddish poet Kadia Molodowsky—

> *O God of Mercy*
> *For the time being*
> *Choose another people*

—and was allowing the Jews to become human beings more or less like anyone else.[1]

But inevitably this meant a relaxation of the burning hope and eagerness which had been, only a generation before, the chief characteristics of the Lower East Side. The once powerfully Jewish trade unions were far less Jewish now. The once militantly Jewish Communist cells had mostly been dissolved. Yiddish itself was gradually being abandoned—fewer and fewer writers thought it worth their while to use it, and the readership of the *Forward* grew older every year. Yet it was all quite fresh in the memory in 1945. If you were not old enough actually to remember the great immigrations, you were certainly old enough to have heard, probably all too often, your parents' memories of them, and very likely to have suffered their overwhelming ambition to get you yourself up in the world, out of the ghetto, beyond the call of pogrom and sweatshop alike.

---

[1] The prayer is translated by Irving Howe in his *World of Our Fathers* (1976), an incomparable account of Jewish immigration to which I am indebted for much of this section.

Many of the heroes of that heroic age were still alive and honored. They included writers like Sholem Asch, Shmuel Niger, I. B. Singer or Abraham Cahan (whose long editorship of the *Forward* had made him a prophet-like arbiter of manners and morals among the Lower East Siders), besides world-famous stars of the theatre and the concert hall such as Jan Peerce (*né* Jacob Perelmuth), Richard Tucker (*né* Reuben Ticker) or Sophie Tucker (*née* Sophia Abuza[1]). The early lyrics of Irving Berlin (*né* Isidore Baline) had included "Yiddishe Eyes" ("Oy, oy, oy, those Yiddishe eyes"); the comedian George Burns had begun as a member of a Lower East Side children's combo called the Pee Wee Quartette; Eddie Cantor had spent half his childhood, he said, sneaking free seats in the theatres of the Rialto, waiting till the crowds came out at intermission time, finding himself an empty seat when they returned.

All these celebrities, and many, many more, were fondly remembered on the Lower East Side, and perhaps the recollection of them, if it gave pride to the neighborhood, also gave it a kind of sadness. Never again, people felt, would their society burn as brightly as that, or throw such glittering particles into the world. But there was a far greater sadness, too, hanging over those shabby fateful streets in the summer of 1945. Happy in general though the denouement of the Jewish immigration had been, its people were grief-stricken now by the knowledge of the European Holocaust,

---

[1] And *morte*, 1966, "The Last of the Red-Hot Mommas."

whose dreadful images were only revealing themselves in that summer of 1945. History had expunged for ever the Jewish communities of eastern Europe whose synagogues, charitable societies and even ghettos had, at so far a remove, implanted their traditions in New York. Thousands of Manhattan Jews had lost relatives in Europe, and even those who had not, whose families had managed to transfer themselves complete to the New World, had lost something almost as precious: their past.

Ghosts of many kinds, then, ghosts blithe enough, ghosts poignant, ghosts utterly tragic, haunted those few streets of the Lower East Side, between Mulberry and Delancey, and over to Second Avenue.[1]

---

[1] Parts of the Lower East Side have now been demolished for housing developments, and the area is only 25 percent Jewish by population, having been infiltrated in later years by Puerto Ricans and Chinese, together with shifting communities of hippies, flower people, punks and yuppies. However much of it is still Jewish-owned, and some of its institutions survive, including two of the most famous, the Educational Alliance and the Henry Street Settlement. Several derelict synagogues have lately been restored, and there are a number of new "storefront synagogues" of fundamentalist Jews. The *Forward* is published from midtown premises now, and its old offices are occupied by a Chinese development company, though the word *Forverts* may still be seen in terracotta Hebrew lettering on its parapet. The Cafe Royal is a dry cleaners. As to New York Jewishness in general, in *Children of the Gilded Ghetto* (1961), by Judith Kramer and Seymour Levantman, a parent is quoted as saying: "I don't want my children to get too much religious training—just enough to know what religion they aren't observing."

The Chinese

Across the road from the Jewish quarter was one of the smallest, tightest and most obvious of the ethnic neighbourhoods, Chinatown. There were perhaps 20,000 Chinese in the whole New York area, but much the best-known of them were the six thousand who lived cheek-by-jowl in the triangular area of five city blocks around Pell, Doyers and Mott Streets, on the edge of the downtown financial district. Most of them or their fore-bears had originally come, it was said, via California from the same district of Toishan in Canton province. For years their jam-packed little enclave had been one of the sights of town, helped by the popular convention, assiduously propagated in those days by Hollywood and strip cartoon, that Chinese people were terribly sinister. O. O. McIntyre had called Chinatown "a faked-up hocus-pocus for yap wagons"; when the sightseeing buses went down there from midtown their passengers were darkly warned to stay close together, holding hands, ladies to walk on the inside of the sidewalk, gentlemen next to the curb—raising in their minds agreeable conjectures of opium den, gang war and white slavery.

In fact Chinatown in 1945 was quite harmless. The secret societies which really had, in previous decades, indulged themselves in racket, gamble and murder, had mostly reverted to their original roles as benevolent fraternities, and a worthy body called the Chinese Consolidated Benevolent Society now kept them all in order, at least in theory. The real interest of the place was its existence as an almost entirely unsullied deposit of Chineseness in the very middle of the downtown city —sticking resolutely to its own ways, and remaining far more Chinese than the Jews of the Lower East Side were Jewish, or even perhaps than the Harlemites were black. There were bigger Chinatowns in the United States, but none were so absolute, or so surprising.

Still surprising, though it was half a century and more since reporters from neighboring newspaper offices had first made the restaurants of Mott Street popular. Chinatown could still take you aback. One minute you were walking down Canal Street, a very characteristic thoroughfare of lower Manhattan, where you might hear the accents of a dozen nations, see the features of a dozen races, all half-subsumed within the American consumer society. The next, and you were over the road in the Orient. One hardly heard an English phrase, or saw an English announcement in Manhattan's China-town then. It was a pure distillation of China—the varnished ducks hanging in open shop-fronts, the smells of spice and cooking, the buckets of crabs clinging to-gether outside fish shops, the old women in their slip-slop slippers, the bright-lit bare-tabled cafes, the phar-macies full of queer medicinal roots and the shambling, colorful, crowded, shelf-cluttered and tumultuous pro-vision stores.

Of all the Manhattan minorities, the Chinese were the most self-contained, if only because very few of them spoke English, and because their enclave seemed to be more or less static—in 1945 the United States's annual quota for Chinese immigrants was 105, which meant that very little new blood found its way down here. They kept themselves to themselves. They had their own banks, their own schools, their own newspapers, their own movie theatre, their own restaurants of course (only some of which were willing to serve chop suey or fortune cookies, those all-American contributions to the Chinese cuisine . . .).

Poking and diffidently exploring around this neighbourhood, which seemed on the face of it indifferent to the curiosity of tourists, the outsider could find many esoteric fascinations. For example at 13 Mott Street the smallest U.S. post office in Manhattan, presided over by a middle-aged lady called Mai Que Cheng, opened directly into the family temple, hung with prayer-papers, thick with incense, in which one might glimpse through a curtain the postmistress's aged mother murmuring her devotions in the half-light. Up the road at number 32 was Quong Yuen Shing, an old general store famous to all Chinese Americans: they used it as a mailing address, a meeting-place and a social center, and at weekends Chinese from all over the country assembled there to exchange views and reminiscences, to pick up a duck or swap an ancient remedy.[1] You could buy snakes

---

[1] The post office at number 13 is now a restaurant. Quong Yuen Shing, which was founded in 1891, claims to be the oldest store in Chinatown, and offers nowadays, besides Chinese turnips and hairy squash, all manner of oriental bric-a-brac.

in Chinatown—steeped alive in rice wine, they made a useful specific against rheumatism—or wildcats which were reduced into a tonic soup. You could read the news from China in a variety of newspapers stuck up on city walls, some presenting the Kuomintang point of view, some the Communist. You could kill four or five hours at a Chinese opera. You could even meet a genuine American missionary—Miss Elizabeth Banta of the True Light Lutheran Church, who had worked for her faith in Chinatown since 1904 precisely as she might have worked in Hangchow or Peking.

The Chinese of Chinatown were extremely clannish. Even their banks were, as often as not, founded upon family arrangements, and were linked still with the far-off villages of Canton whence these recondite New Yorkers had come. They were a mystery and a marvel. To their neighbors over on Canal Street or Delancey they seemed altogether inaccessible, to the tourists from uptown they were wonderfully arcane: yet across the wildly variegated rooftops of their quarter the tower of the Woolworth Building, one of the most unmistakably American of all artifacts, looked down paternally upon the goings-on.[1]

---

[1] And could those Chinese but have known it, theirs was to prove the most successful of all these neighbourhoods. Forty years later, the immigration quota having been lifted, their community had boldly burst the bounds of Chinatown and spread far to the north and east, while the original triangle of the quarter boomed

All the World

Chinatown, the old Jewish quarter, Harlem—they were the three most evident and celebrated of Manhattan's ethnic neighbourhoods. But everywhere else on the island too racial enclaves of one kind or another were expanding or decreasing, fermenting or quiescent, lying low or asserting themselves, accepting the propositions of the Melting Pot or propagating its sociological rival of the time, Cultural Pluralism. Seen with a divine eye, from a height even greater than the Empire State's, the island must have looked like a demographic volcano, latent for the moment perhaps but decidedly not extinct.

Some of the oldest ethnic groups had almost vanished. The American Indians, the oldest of them all, showed themselves by 1945 only as steeplejacks and construction workers (they had particularly good heads for heights) and the nearest reserves, the Shinnecock and the Poosepatuck, were sixty miles away at the far end of Long Island. The Dutch, the founders of the city, had been reduced to a kind of spectral eminence: old Dutch names still carried social weight, but the very last of the New York Stuyvesants, whose forebear the one-legged

---

as never before. There are said to be 300 garment factories in the area, and 150 eating-places, most of which will probably give you chop suey if you ask.

Peter had been the most famous of the Dutch governors, was even then awaiting his burial in the family vault at St. Mark's-in-the-Bouwerie, on Second Avenue at 10th Street.[1] The English had generally just become Americans, but of the eighteen other peoples said to have been represented in the Manhattan of Peter Stuyvesant's time, and the many more whose emissaries came later, most were still recognizably half-themselves.

The Irish, who had more or less run the city until recent years, were scattered all over it socially—there never had been an Irish quarter—but concentrated vocationally as policemen, politicians, railroad men, bartenders, publicans and drivers of Central Park horse-cabs: their St. Patrick's Day parade was the biggest parade of all, and old Irish ladies of Manhattan still sometimes curtseyed when a priest went by. The Italians, though they still had a fiercely Italian quarter around Mulberry Street, between the Chinese and the Jews, were dispersed all over the city too, and their reputation ran the whole Italianate gamut, from the folksy familial, all mamas and homemade pasta, to the Sicilian conspiratorial, all vendettas and submachine guns. The Germans were concentrated around Yorkville, on the Upper East Side, where they had their own clubs, newspapers and brewery, where fräuleins in

---

[1] It was not to happen until 1953, when he became the eighty-fifth inhabitant of the vault. In the meantime Augustus Van Horn Stuyvesant was driven down there once or twice a month, in his venerable Rolls-Royce, to meditate among the tombstones.

aprons served Black Forest cake and Bavarian sauer-
braten at the Cafe Geiger, where you could eat veal
goulash at Kleine Konditorei, or drink frothy lager out
of pewter-lidded beer steins at many a cellar tavern (and
where before the war the Nazis had not been universally
unpopular . . .).

There was a little Spain on West 14th Street, speaking Castilian, though Galicians and Catalans preferred
to congregate near Brooklyn Bridge, speaking Catalan
and Galician. Armenians and Turks did their best to
keep clear of each other, especially on All-Armenian
Martyrs' Day (the Armenians had an elegant cathedral
on Second Avenue, the Turks had to go to Brooklyn to
find a mosque). There were Russians of several kinds—
Russian Jews of course, but also White Russians, whose
best-known area of settlement was the cluster of expensive apartment houses on midtown Fifth Avenue,
whence they sauntered ever and again into dinner party
and gossip column. Two Russian cathedrals rivalled one
another, and in midtown there were two well-known
Russian restaurants, the Russian Tea Room which had
been founded (by a Pole, actually) in 1928, and the
Russian Bear which offered the homesick émigré every
possible Russian consolation, whether it was samovar
tea he wanted, or excellent house vodka, or balalaika
music, or the services of an experienced palmiste.[1]
Gypsies of several national origins lived in scattered

---

[1] The Russian Bear has since closed, but the Russian Tea Room
still obliges.

groups, inhabiting the very worst tenements, nearly all illiterate and alas given to petty crime (one city detective worked entirely on gypsy malfeasance). Most of them still spoke Romany, and their children helped the family finances by tap dancing in saloons; when they needed funerals or marriages they went to the Orthodox church of St. Peter and Paul on East 7th Street, or the nearby Catholic church of St. Stanislaus, led often by one of the gypsy kings whose monarchies proliferated.

All the world was there—almost all the world, for there were very few Asian Indians in Manhattan (though Indian chefs had long been cooking the celebrated curries of the Pierre Hotel), very few Arabs, surprisingly few South Americans, and only two resident Dusuns from North Borneo (one of whom, said to be recently descended from head-hunters, kept a barber's shop on Amsterdam Avenue).

It Worked!

What was more extraordinary still was the way these several communities had managed to ride out the atavistic differences savaging the rest of the world. Doubtless there had been nationalistic tensions among the neighbourhoods during the war—"Put out your lights, you Nazi Fascist Germans!" screams a woman during the dim-out in one of John Cheever's stories. With the coming of peace they were soon forgotten. You would hardly know, as they celebrated the great victory on the Upper East Side, that Germans had been enemies at all, and the fact that Italy had been at war with the United States seemed to have been put entirely out of mind on Mulberry Street. German-ness, Italian-ness were nothing to be ashamed of. There were innumerable German and Italian names, after all, on the roll call of the *Queen Mary*; among the national heroes of the day were Frank Sinatra, Joe DiMaggio and General Eisenhower himself. Even the Japanese, so harshly used elsewhere in America, were not entirely stigmatized in New York. Throughout the war Miyako's Restaurant on West 56th had served dinner in entirely Japanese style, as it had since 1910, and the Japanese Buddhist temple on West 94th Street, with its black and gold shrine from Kyoto, its free Japanese language lessons and its demonstrations of flower arrangements and calligraphy, had been left without interference, as though Pearl Harbor and Wake Island, Guadalcanal and the Solomons had never happened at all.[1]

A familiar War Bond poster, stuck up all over Manhattan, showed a happy immigrant family smiling out

---

[1] Today Western-style Japanese restaurants are on every other Manhattan corner, but in the front room of Miyako's, almost alone in midtown, you may still eat on the floor.

at passers-by above the following text: "If my father hadn't come to America about 35 years ago, I'd be starving in Poland . . . I'd be sobbing in France . . . I'd be stealing in Greece . . . I'd be shivering in Belfast . . . I'd be slaving in Frankfurt . . . I'd be hiding in Prague . . . I'd be buried in Russia." Manhattan in 1945 was conscious of its luck, and proud of its purpose as a haven. It was one place left in the world where Jews and Germans lived side by side, Turks and Armenians at least co-existed, Chinese drank their healthful wildcat soup while gypsies down the road got married in churches of St. Stanislaus, and even the little yellow men with slit eyes and cruel smiles so often anathematized in the movies were still recognized as humans. It worked! The English writer Cecil Roberts, who had spent the war years in Manhattan, reported that on the five floors of his apartment house there lived an Austrian doctor, a Lithuanian politician, a Dutch artist, a Polish rabbi, a Turkish broadcaster, a cousin of the Shah of Persia, an American-Armenian, a Cuban pianist, an Australian nurse, a Spanish shipping agent and a German-born art dealer.

And even in that moment of hiatus the celestial viewer, watching from high above, might detect the simmerings of yet another ethnic eruption in Manhattan. The immigration laws did not affect newcomers who were already American citizens, and a vast new multitude of immigrants from the newly emancipated Commonwealth of Puerto Rico was even then about to invade the city to change things once again——bringing just the same hopes, arousing just the same prejudices as so many newcomers before them, and doubtless settling into Manhattan's microcosm of the world just as naturally in the end.[1]

---

[1] In 1940 there had been 40,000 Puerto Ricans in New York, by 1954 there were 450,000. In 1946 a new influx of European immigrants began to arrive, too, out of the displaced persons camps, and in 1967 the abolition of the quota system opened the doors at last to Oriental immigrants. Today Koreans appear to own half the grocery stores, Indians and Pakistanis run nearly all the news-stands, and I would think that Manhattan in 1987 is more vividly cosmopolitan than it has ever been. Whether the Melting Pot or Cultural Pluralism is winning the old rivalry seems to me anyone's guess.

4

On Class

ON THE HIGH BREEZY RIDGE of Morningside Heights (altitude 250 feet at least) there stood a rich and splendid group of monumental buildings. There were two theological colleges, one Jewish (the Jewish Theological Seminary of America, with the world's greatest collection of Hebraica), the other Christian (the Union Theological Seminary, so influential it was said that to find a parallel "perhaps one would have to go back to Geneva in the time of Calvin"[1]). There was Riverside Church, where the world's most famous carillonneur played the world's largest carillon. There was the sumptuous unfinished Cathedral of St. John the Divine, whose marble

---

[1] David Gourlay, in *Cousins and Strangers*, 1956.

columns had been quarried in Maine, shipped in on
barges at enormous expense and dragged through the
Manhattan streets by steam winch. And all around were
the quadrangles, libraries and laboratories of Columbia
University, one of Manhattan's richest landlords, whose
properties included the site of Rockefeller Center.

Immediately to the east of these opulent institutions,
almost symbolically surveyed by the tower of Riverside
Church down the line of West 121st Street, and by Dr.
Butler's presidential mansion on the ridge, Morningside
Park fell away steep, gloomy and dangerous after dark
directly into Harlem. It was only a few minutes' walk
from those splendors to the hugger-mugger squalors of
the black slums. The contrast was bitter, and all too
explicit.[1] It was however by no means an extreme example of social confrontation in Manhattan. In many
parts of this island very rich people were living almost
side by side with exceedingly poor, and there was hardly
such a thing as an exclusive quarter.[2] Tenements were
just around the corner from luxury blocks; a few hundred yards separated Beekman Place, one of the very

---

[1] So explicit that twenty years later the Episcopalian bishop announced the suspension of building work on the Cathedral—
construction funds would be used to alleviate the neighbouring
poverty instead. But by 1978 the cathedral-builders were back in
business.

[2] Though in general the East Side was thought much smarter than
the West. Son on the telephone: "Dad, you gotta come and help
me, they've arrested me for armed robbery on the West Side."
Father: "Good God, son, what were you doing over there?"

grandest of the East Side residential addresses, from the riverside tanneries and slaughterhouses of Turtle Bay, where on any weekday morning the animals could be seen driven from truck to charnel. This social promiscuity was inevitable, with 1.8 million people crammed into 14,000 acres. Manhattan was a city in the round, without suburbs on the island, made all the more absolute by the narrowness of its limits. It was the richest of cities, with some of the most dismal slums. It was elegant and it was scruffy. It was vociferously democratic, but also decidedly oligarchal. It was all things to all classes.

Around the 400

Here as everywhere war had discredited social distinctions, and weakened some of the assumptions that Americans had inherited, against all the intentions of their founding fathers, from the societies of Europe. Nevertheless at the top of the heap a remnant of New York's prewar social Old Guard flourished loftily still. It was not so long since the mansions along Fifth Avenue, from the 30s up to the 70s and beyond, had one and all been private houses, and some still were.

At the corner of 75th Street Mrs. Edward Harkness, widow of a cultivated midwest millionaire, lived in Renaissance grandeur behind an iron-spiked fence, surrounded by servants—maids on the fifth floor, men-servants in the basement. At the corner of 79th Street lived that last of the Stuyvesants, Augustus Van Horne the property millionaire, alone with his butler, his valet, his chaffeur and his housekeeping staff. At the corner of 61st Street, number 800, which looked entirely abandoned, was in fact the thirty-five-roomed occasional pied-à-terre of Mrs. Marcellus Hartley Dodge, whose innumerable dogs had their kennels on the fifth floor.

At number 972 was Mrs. Helen Payne Whitney, widowed heiress to $178 million, with the cherry and black racing colors of the Whitney stables flying from the roof. At the corner of 92nd Street lived the bachelor playboy John Jacob Astor and his twenty-five servants. In the library of her house on the corner of 51st Street, almost opposite St. Patrick's, Mrs. Cornelius Vanderbilt was At Home each evening, with her statutory four red roses in their four silver vases, her candles burning beside the long mirror, a Turner landscape on one wall, on another a seventeenth-century tapestry, and beside the roaring log fire, if the season was right, tea from a silver service for her usual assortment of diplomats, maharajahs, admirals, local swells and foreign royalty— as she remarked to a visiting Englishman once, "I have known personally three of your kings."[1] Though many

---

[1] The house was demolished that year—it was on the corner of the Rockefeller Center site—and Mrs. Vanderbilt moved to a slightly more modest home, higher up the Avenue, where for some time things went on much the same. The interior of her old library was sold to Paramount Films, who used it as a set.

another palace had been torn down or turned into museum, store or apartment block, people still called midtown Fifth Avenue Millionaires' Row, and some of the horse cab drivers who took tourists for trots around Central Park claimed to have been coachmen to great families of Manhattan's legendary 400.

Four hundred souls were supposed to have been as many as could be entertained, sixty years before, in the legendary drawing-room of Mrs. Caroline Schermerhorn Astor, whose husband was the great-grandson of a German butcher but who herself claimed descent from Scottish kings. It had therefore become the traditional quota of utterly socially acceptable New Yorkers, as listed in the *Social Register*. To get into the Register, which had been published annually since 1886, you either proposed yourself, presenting your pedigree and giving as references six people already in the book, or you "married into the Register," as the saying was. (But when Gene Tunney the boxer, a most gentlemanly man, married a Register-listed bride, instead of including him they dropped her. A sceptic called Francis Crowinshield, in his book *Manners for the Metropolis*, suggested a more honest method of selection, based upon points: six for the possession of an opera box, five for a steam yacht, two for each million dollars in the bank, half a point for each identifiable grandparent . . .)

By 1945 the Register contained far more than 400 names, but there were still people who regarded it as a true gauge of social worth, and families who greatly prided themselves upon the magic letters "Myf," discreetly printed beside their entries, which showed their alleged descent from Pilgrims on the *Mayflower*. Many of the names would have been familiar enough, too, to Mrs. Caroline Schermerhorn Astor. Eight of her own clan were listed. So of course was Mr. A. Van Horne Stuyvesant. Nine Vanderbilts were there, and there were fifteen Rockefellers. The Rockefeller dynasty was supreme in Manhattan by then, having not only given the city the eponymous Center, but also endowed the Museum of Modern Art, the Cloisters Museum, the Riverside Church and the Rockefeller Institute for Medical Research: even so, the Register pedantically refused to list the family patriarch as John D. Rockefeller, Jr., as he endearingly preferred to call himself in deference to his departed dad.[1]

Millionaires' Row and all it represented had been badly shaken first by the advent of income tax, then by the Depression, and finally by the war, but many New Yorkers still lived as grandly as ever. Their butlers were still to be seen exercising the dogs in the park; their European nannies still paraded young masters and

---

[1] The *Social Register* is still going strong, still advises its readers "If the married name you are seeking has escaped your memory and you can recall the maiden name, reference to the Married Maidens will then indicate the present name," and now gives you a little yacht symbol if you own a yacht. In 1985, by my bemused count, it numbered two Astors, ten Vanderbilts and twenty-eight Rockefellers—who had since made a gift to the world of the United Nations site on the East River. Alas, by then no Stuyvesants were in the book.

misses around the boating pool; their chauffeurs wore leather leggings, double-breasted jackets (Mr. Stuyvesant's was dressed all in plum), and sometimes the stylishly tucked white scarves given chic by the United States Army. Their snobbery could still be excruciating —at the Metropolitan Opera there were fashionable and unfashionable boxes, the ones on the south side being the more desirable. Even the general move into apartments had not necessarily restrained their style, for their new quarters could be almost as palatial as their old: Marjorie Meriwether Post the cereal heiress and her husband E. F. Hutton had fifty-four rooms in their three-story apartment at 1107 Fifth Avenue.

Among the Old Families, as they liked to call themselves, few of the pre-war conventions had been abandoned, from the annual summer migration to Newport or Nantucket to the series of winter balls, mostly in the ballroom of the Plaza Hotel, at which they presented their daughters to society. Upon the Grosvenor Ball, the Gotham Ball, the Junior League Ball, even in 1945, many a Manhattan girl believed her whole future happiness to depend. The most successful of the debutantes were celebrities, seldom absent from the gossip columns, almost household names in fact (two of the most prominent of the prewar comers-out, Brenda Frazier and Cobina Wright, Jr., had even achieved the distinction of parody by the comedian Bob Hope, in the personae of distinctly un-Registered ladies from Brooklyn). At the end of the worst of wars there was no European social protocol to match all this, not even in England; the foreign aristocrats who frequented these Manhattan milieux, varying as they did from Dukes of Windsor to debatably authenticated Italian counts, were often astonished by the formality of everything, often envious one supposes, and perhaps just occasionally mocking.

Club Life

Women played the major part in these nonsensicals, and the local upper-crust ladies had created social patterns all their own. By the standards of the day feminism was powerful in this city—the phrase "male chauvinist" had already been used here. Manhattan women were famously independent, and famously "smart." Some truly formidable women had fought their way to influence in business and finance, and in general educated women in Manhattan were more emancipated than their sisters almost anywhere else. Bars still sometimes declined to serve them, it was true, but even that resilient prejudice had been weakened by the pressures of Prohibition, and it was many long years since the actress Lily Langtry, refused ale and a mutton chop at Keen's chophouse, had taken the management to court, and won.[1]

---

[1] "Ladies are in luck!" the restaurant promptly and astutely advertised. "They can now dine at Keen's!"

Innumerable women's organizations sustained this liberty, bolstered the sense of feminine power, satisfied *amour-propre*, provided cultural uplift, offered professional support or fulfilled charitable leanings. The most famous of the "ghoulish sororities," as Henry Miller once called them, were the Colonial Dames of America, whose members must trace their ancestry back to pre-Revolutionary times, and the Daughters of the American Revolution, whose pedigrees need not be *quite* so long, but should in theory be more republican: but there were also women's social clubs (the extremely posh Colony, the more intellectual Cosmopolitan) of a sophistication, luxury and confidence beyond anything achieved by European women. The female governing class of Manhattan was, in short, *sui generis*. Its style was inimitably American, and though its members often prided themselves, even Daughters of the Revolution, on mistily-traced descent from earls or baronets, their social affairs were really as American as could be.

Not so the club life of their husbands, for the male social associations of Manhattan were based all too obviously on London models, and often seemed to younger English visitors, indeed, like relics of a lost London age, or fictions from a Jamesian novel. Some were enormously expensive and horribly exclusive (Jews not welcome, let alone blacks): the Metropolitan Club at Fifth Avenue and 60th had been founded by J. P. Morgan allegedly for friends blackballed elsewhere, but was by now extremely choosy itself. Some were deliberately informal. At the Brook Club, which was founded in 1904 and was very like London's Beefsteak Club, members dined at a communal table and were expected to talk to whatever member they found next to them (the club motto was "Men may come and men may go, but I go on for ever"). At the Coffee House luncheon club the only rule was that there were no rules, while we are told that at meetings of the peripatetic club called The Occasional Thinkers even Dr. Nicholas Murray Butler, there nicknamed The Sage, was induced to lead the members in "college songs, songs of bygone periods, and original songs about members of the group." Some clubs were nothing if not stately of environment, like the Racquet and Tennis Club in its Tuscan palace on Park Avenue, or the University on Fifth Avenue, whose members ate their breakfasts in a kind of cathedral. Others again were boyishly clubbable, in a way almost forgotten in England. As it happened the Century Association, on West 43rd Street, was soon to celebrate its first centenary in a manner very characteristic of this last trait; so perhaps its committee will forgive us if, purely for literary purposes, we gate-crash the occasion.

The Century had been founded specifically for "authors, artists and amateurs of the fine arts," and the Centurions, as they called themselves, included many famous men, the vast majority bearing Anglo-Saxon names. Theirs was a club of stylish tradition. Its servants, so its chairman said in his centenary message to the members, were "an essential part of the friendship that reigns in our home," and in fact the Head Billiards Marker had been with the club for forty-nine years. On

Centenary Night the friendship was even more apparent than usual. The splendid clubhouse, built in 1891, was open to women for the evening, and was ablaze with light. Festive noises rang up and down 43rd Street, and outside the front door an ambulance stood, in case merriment went too far.

Through the great doors we go, up the marble staircase, and we find the whole solemn building given over to hilarity (except for the first aid room, where two Centurion surgeons are standing by, linked by radio with that ambulance). Everywhere people in tuxedos and long dresses are laughing, dancing, loudly talking, eating, sitting in corners drinking, calling to each other across enormous rooms, telling old stories and introducing wives to one another. In the library they are serving punch and hot dogs. On the fourth floor Harry Bennet, Centurion, is playing the piano, surrounded by a swinging, singing crowd. The focus of the celebrations is a pageant enacting the history of the club, with a procession through the clubhouse to the music of "O God Our Help in Ages Past," led by an elder holding the Silver Column of the Century with its lighted lamp, and attended by dancing elves. There is a declamatory poem by Christopher La Farge, and a playlet by Thornton Wilder portraying the club "as our sons imagine it" (stuffy), "as a new member imagines it" (daunting), and "as our wives imagine it" (dissolute). They play it three times that night; at ten o'clock the audience is decorous, but by the midnight showing it is officially described as being composed "entirely of howling dervishes."

It is a very jolly, very carefree, intensely fraternal scene. Much drink is drunk. Many laughs are laughed. A lot of hot dogs are eaten. Mr. Bennet plays his piano indefatigably until the first daylight creeps through the clubhouse windows, and the last of the revellers disperses to breakfast. At 5:30 a.m. the ambulance turns off its radio and goes home too, its services not having been required.[1]

Cafe Society

Around the perimeter of the allegorical 400, sometimes overlapping, sometimes shying away, there was something called Cafe Society. This was a public rather than a private organism, highly visible, whose activities were recorded faithfully by the gossip writers, and whose members were a mixture of old family, screen and theatre people, musicians, sportsmen, actors, some writers,

---

[1] The Century Association, all the same, was not without its inner controversies. It had been split by the election to membership of a Communist economist, who was alleged to have said during a political campaign that politics was "the science of who gets what, when and how." Forty years later it was again divided, this time by the issue of female membership (resisted by most of its members), but it remains one of the most distinguished and clubbable of Manhattan clubs.

with a sprinkling of foreign patricians and a new stratum of sufficiently fashionable military men. If in some ways it was the New York equivalent of Evelyn Waugh's Bright Young Things in London before the war, in others it was a foretaste of Jet Sets yet to come.

It had a slightly nostalgic air, looking back as it did to racier times—times of Cole Porter and the Gershwin brothers, of the Cotton Club in Harlem, of Prohibition and its reckless excitements, times when one went out in one's Packard, loaded with flowers and booze, to see one's friends off on the Pan Am Clipper to Europe, exaggerated times, when Peggy Hopkins Joyce had her gloves made with extra large third fingers to accommodate her diamonds, and Woolworth Donahue the prankster of pranksters—remember Woolworth?—got up to all those *crazy* tricks . . .

All this was faded rather, but a sort of miasma of the Cafe Society, with its undertones of the past, still hung around Manhattan. In particular perhaps it pervaded the great hotels of the city, for its habitués had always loved grand hotels, and grand hotels had enthusiastically catered for them—was it not to a suite at the Plaza that the Great Gatsby and his friends resorted, when they could think of nothing else to do? The Manhattan hotel had always been something rather different from its equivalents elsewhere. Thousands of Manhattan families lived permanently in hotels—sometimes apartment hotels, with kitchens, often just plain hotels, where they depended upon room service or in-house restaurants. But people also looked to hotels as natural centers of social life; even in 1795, when Manhattan extended no further north than Wall Street, the City Hotel at 115 Broadway had been one of the most imposing buildings in town, and it was to be followed by an endlessly famous succession of prodigies—the Fifth Avenue Hotel, the Astor, the St. Regis, the Waldorf—all in their days supremely sumptuous and gregarious.

In the 1940s the city's selection of first-rate hotels was unequalled in the world. They were all extremely expensive, especially to foreign visitors travelling on devalued currencies, but they varied greatly in ambience. The Plaza beside the park was the *grande dame* of them all (though it was less than forty years old); afternoon tea at the Plaza was one of Manhattan society's diurnal engagements. The old-fashioned Brevoort on lower Fifth Avenue was beloved of the old school too; it was the first Manhattan establishment to put cafe tables on its sidewalk, and had a leisurely European feel. The Biltmore, whose lower ground floor actually connected to the upper arrival platform of Grand Central, was the national headquarters of the Democratic Party; it had a chapel in it (Room 300), and was popular with academics, who were often said by snide colleagues to have been "working in the library at the Biltmore." The Pierre and the Carlyle were suave newcomers. The St. Regis had a reputation for high jinks. The Ritz-Carlton on Madison Avenue was said by insiders to be the snootiest of them all. Such hotels were swish but not starchy—the very luxurious Sherry Netherlands did not mind figuring in Pepsi-Cola advertisements—and they offered not only bars, restaurants and shops, but famous entertainment too, ranging from Myru, The Wizard of Mental Telepathy, who was appearing in cabaret at the Pierre that summer, to Glenn Miller, who had made the very telephone number of the Statler famous with his hit song *"PEnnsylvania Six Five Thousand."*[1]

In 1945 the Waldorf-Astoria was their summation, and its saloon called Peacock Alley, off the foyer, was a favorite gathering-place of Cafe Society's survivors. The hotel was actually divided into two parts, the hotel proper and the more discreet Waldorf Towers, where people like the Windsors and President Hoover maintained permanent apartments, but in the general mind it was one enormous block of luxurious exclusivity. It had been built in the early 1930s to replace the old Waldorf-Astoria on Fifth Avenue, demolished to make way for the Empire State Building, and it stood above the subterranean railroad tracks of Park Avenue.

Everything about it was splashy. Its twin towers were the thirteenth tallest in Manhattan, and between them was strung a festoon of radio aerials, feeding what was described in the hotel brochures as the world's largest private radio station. Its ballroom, rising four stories in the heart of the building, was claimed to be the most

---

[1] Still its number, translated as 736-5000, though the hotel is now called the Penta. The Brevoort and the Biltmore have gone now, and the present Ritz-Carlton is a later incarnation of the name; the other hotels mentioned here have maintained their personalities to this day.

magnificent room ever built in a hotel. The Starlight Roof slid open to the stars when the weather was right. The Waldorf-Astoria's plan allowed people to drive their cars into the very middle of the structure, where there was an inner courtyard; but undoubtedly *the* way to arrive was in one's private railroad car, which could be shunted off the New York Central's main line into private sidings deep below the hotel.[1]

Though the Waldorf (as it was generally called) was enormous—1800 rooms on forty-seven stories—the management tried to make the hotel exclusive in the European kind. The task was approached methodically, and a multivolumed manual of instruction provided guidance exact and all-embracing. When a patron arrived at the front desk, for example, "the clerk's keen appraisal should determine whether to make this transaction efficient, courteous and brief, or make it a dramatic moment for the patron." Floor clerks (there was one to each floor) must say "Please" and "Thank you" to patrons regularly and sincerely, while never becoming chatty—"Talkativeness is bad form and entirely out of place." "Remember that every word uttered to a patron is regarded by the patron as a statement from the Wal-

---

[1] The tracks are still there, rumbled past by the trains on their way to Grand Central up the way, and at the side of the hotel, on 49th Street, you may see the big bronze doors which used to give access to the hotel's private arrival platform. Nobody comes that way now, but a railway wagon down there contains the hotel's surplus stock of china.

dorf. The patron puts up the money that supports the Waldorf—and you."[1]

The Waldorf was one of the supreme Manhattan institutions. *Weekend at the Waldorf*, a frothy comedy set in the hotel, was released to the movie houses that very year, and many a hero of the late war—Eisenhower, De Gaulle, Bradley, Nimitz, Halsey—was honoured at a Waldorf banquet. Among the resident guests in the first postwar months were Prince Aksel of Denmark, Prince Sibha Svasti of Siam, Prince Feisal of Saudi Arabia, Princess Pearl, daughter of the Rajah of Sarawak, and the Marquess of Queensberry, described by the hotel's publicity man as Hereditary King of Scotland, and so presumably related to the late Mrs. Astor. At a luncheon for Charles de Gaulle, August 27, 1945, Mlle. Marcella Denya of the Paris Opera sang the French national anthem, Mrs. Helen Jepson of the Metropolitan Opera, the American. When Winston Churchill was given a banquet in the following year, the pudding was Bombe Glace Britannia.[2]

---

[1] My favorite instruction in this enthralling handbook reads as follows: "Clowning at work: Clowning on the premises is forbidden."

[2] On the typed printer's copy of the menu which I have before me now, the words "Hine Cognac" have been hastily pencilled in beside the demitasse: perhaps somebody had looked up the guest of honor's preferences in the Patrons' History Division—a type of personal service, says the manual, which "appeals to visitors and makes them loyal patrons and boosters." The Waldorf, now part of the Hilton group, celebrated its fiftieth anniversary in 1981:

Celebrity-Spotting

Celebrities were the pillars of Cafe Society—perhaps even of Manhattan society really. It was no good being rich and well-born if, like Mrs. Dodge, you lived all alone in your mansion with your dogs, or simply appeared once a month to prearrange your funeral, like Mr. Stuyvesant. Fortunately Manhattan in 1945 was absolutely stuffed with celebrities. Some had been there always, some had gravitated there during the war, and many more now came pouring into the city which, more lavishly than any other in the world, offered the prizes of fame.

Just as nowhere in Manhattan were you far from some glorious artistic treasure, flaunted in museum or gloated over in private house, so there was no moment, at least in midtown, where you could not hope to see a celebrity. If you did not know where to start, the gossip columnists would help. "Bumped into Brenda Frazier at El Morocco last night," they would tell you confidentially, or "They say Tony's Trouville is the 'in' place this season." At Sardi's restaurant on West 44th Street you were almost sure to see somebody from Broadway or Hollywood: it had been in the hands of

---

guests at a celebratory banquet were served, among much else, the biggest birthday cake ever made, Goujonettes of Trout rolled in Corn Meal ("as served to President Hoover") and Jelly Beans ("as enjoyed by President and Mrs. Ronald Reagan").

the Sardi family since 1921, and was later to be described as "the club, mess hall, lounge, post office, saloon and marketplace of the people of the theatre."[1] At the El Morocco on East 54th Street you might indeed see Miss Frazier or her friend Cobina—it was there, the *New Yorker* reported that summer, that "the dress-for-dinner contingent is making its last desperate stand." For sporting stars you could try Toots Shor's, on West 52nd Street; Mr. Shor was admired for his apothegm "a bum who ain't drunk by midnight ain't trying," and his restaurant was frequented by the likes of Babe Ruth, Joe DiMaggio and Leo ("Leo the Lip") Durocher, who was admired for *his* apothegm "Nice guys finish last." And for the famous of all kinds, social or artistic, political or financial, there was the 21 Club on 52nd Street. This was not really a club at all, but a former speakeasy, Jack and Charlie's, now run (by Jack Kriendler and Charlie Berns) as a very expensive restaurant. It was a place of private codes—habituées called it The Numbers, or The Three—and fundamentally it was a semi-private society for its regulars, who used it as a home from home. But it was a great place for celebrity-spotting too. Legend said that clients at the 21 were actually seated according to rank of celebrity, the very famous in front, the middle famous by the kitchen door, and the nobodies in a back room known in the vernacular as Siberia. Certainly, as Lawton McKall the restaurant

---

[1] By the press agent Richard Maney when it was sold in 1985 to two Broadway producers.

critic wrote, a stranger trying to get a table there would find that if he had "written a Broadway hit, turned out a best-seller, or scored in the movies, it would advance his cause considerably. . . ."

Jack and Charlie were majordomos of celebrity. The Beau Nash of Manhattan, though, was Sherman Billingsley of the Stork Club. Where but the Stork Club could one see Cobina Wright, "the city's loveliest debutante," in the same room as H. L. Mencken, Madame Chiang Kai-shek, the Duke and Duchess of Windsor or the Ernest Hemingways? Billingsley, known to his often fawning customers as "Sherm," at once basked in their reflected fame and vigorously exploited it. He employed two teams of press agents, one on day shift, one on night, and he assiduously cultivated the friendship of newspaper columnists like Walter Winchell ("the King"), or Leonard Lyons, of "The Lyons Den," who were by then celebrities themselves. Some said he had actually *invented* the Cafe Society; he had first advertised his club in college newspapers, and given publicity to suitably prepossessing and sufficiently moneyed students as "prominent members of Cafe Society."

Billingsley had reached success the hard way, from Enid, Oklahoma, pop. 300, via a series of Bronx drug stores specializing in whiskey prescriptions during Prohibition. He had started his Stork Club as an up-market speakeasy—the first, he used to say, with a carpet on the floor and a canopy out front. By 1945, although the club menu still felt obliged to advise its clients not to drink red wine with fish, and some people took their children to breakfast there after Sunday morning church, it had become a very symbol of Manhattan sophistication. It was "the New Yorkiest place in town," wrote Winchell, who spent every evening at his own Stork Club table, where people lined up to be interviewed by him. "Sherm" himself called it "a place unique to itself— the elite of the world have graced my tables."

Sometimes un-graced them too, for Billingsley, like Nash before him, could be severe upon patrons, however eminent, who misbehaved themselves in his eyes. Sometimes he banned them—Elliot Roosevelt the President's son was a black sheep of the Stork Club, and Humphrey Bogart was another. The Maharajah of Jaipur was once refused entry, on grounds of color. Mr. Billingsley was not averse to such contretemps. Just as Beau Nash is remembered to this day for tearing the apron off the Duchess of Queensberry, when he considered her under-dressed for the Bath Assembly Rooms, so when Sherm gave the thumbs down to another star, or had the golden key of membership thrown back at him by an affronted socialite, there was always Mr. Winchell, Table 50, to put it in his column.[1]

---

[1] Billingsley died in 1966, and his obituary in the *Times* said that by then both he and his club seemed "as square and as outdated as the fox-trot and the waltz." The Stork Club, with murals of top-hatted storks outside its doors, stood on the site now occupied by Paley Park, a diminutive retreat of trees and falling water where Sherm might not have felt entirely at home. Sardi's still exists, the 21 thrives; the present Toots Shor restaurant is not the same place at all.

Some Mavericks

Countless citizens of Manhattan considered themselves outside class, outside convention too, and life for such mavericks was greatly eased by the city's fondness for individuality. At its coarsest this may have been just laissez-faire or no-holds-barred, but in subtler kinds it was an aristocratic recognition of human values. The city had always enjoyed peculiarities of nomenclature and geography—the North River, as its citizens loved to tell out-of-towners, was not in the north, the East River was not a river, Houston Street was inexplicably pronounced Howston and there was a little enclave of Manhattan, Marble Hill, which was not on the island at all, but on the Bronx side of the Harlem River. In just the same way did Manhattan cherish its human exceptions, its show-offs and its oddballs. This was a city of extraordinary people, and it was proud of the fact. All was forgiven a man—well *nearly* all—if he was extraordinary enough. Venal but entertaining politicians, brutal but colorful gangsters, excruciatingly snobby socialites, preposterously vain performers, all found their way to Manhattan's heart, and the city's lore was rich in tales of recluses, exhibitionists and miscellaneous cranks.

For instance a universally welcome figure in Greenwich Village, the more or less literary quarter of town, was the penniless litterateur Joseph Ferdinand Gould, who had been writing for almost as long as anyone could remember a gigantic Oral History of the World. Gould, who was in his fifties, 5'4" tall and a member of the Harvard class of 1911, used to say that he lived on air, self-esteem, coffee, fried-egg sandwiches and ketchup, and claimed to have translated much of Longfellow into the seagull language. With his ivory cigarette-holder, his baggy clothes, his toothless grin, his beard and his bald top, he had been frequenting the bars and cafes of the Village for thirty years and more, and was known to everyone as The Professor.

By 1945 his history, which he was writing in a series of school composition books, is said to have contained at least 9 million longhand words, and most of it had been deposited for safekeeping, in case of air raids, on a Long Island chicken farm. Nobody however had ever read it, and nobody really knew whether it was genius, gibberish or just mediocrity. Gould was treated with affection anyway. He was given free drinks and meals all over the place, and was invited to all the best Village parties, where at the drop of a hat he would recite some well-known poem in seagull. There was perhaps not another metropolis in the world where so apparent a charlatan would have found such generous kindness.[1]

Eccentrics of another kind, almost equally well-known in the Manhattan of 1945, were the Collyer

---

[1] Gould was given a wider and lasting fame by Joseph Mitchell in *McSorley's Wonderful Saloon*. He died in 1957, aged sixty-eight, alas in a hospital for the mentally ill, and what became of his *Oral History* nobody seems to know. Hemingway sent gladioli to his funeral.

brothers, two white men who had lived in Harlem since 1909, when it had been a fashionable white area. They had turned their brownstone house there into a kind of fortress, allowing nobody else into it. Every passage was blocked with immense piles of books and newspapers, through which crawling-tunnels led from room to room. The front door was barricaded with miscellaneous rubbish, and booby-traps were laid here and there inside. There was no gas, electricity, running water or sewage connection, but amidst all the squalor was housed an excellent library, mostly about mechanics and the sea, together with fourteen grand pianos.

Homer Collyer, who was an admiralty lawyer by profession, had been paralyzed since 1932, and was looked after by Langley, a former concert pianist. He lived on a diet of one hundred oranges a week, resting his almost blind eyes, so Langley reported, by keeping them permanently closed. The Collyers were popularly supposed to be enormously wealthy, and often got into the newspapers, but nobody ever interfered with them it seems, or tried to make them live like everyone else. They were the Collyer Brothers, Harlem's Most Fascinating Mystery, as the tabloids liked to say, and fascinatingly mysterious they were allowed to remain.[1]

---

[1] When Homer died in 1947, making the front page of the *New York Times*, it took the police two hours to break into the house with axes and crowbars. Langley had disappeared, but three weeks later he was found dead too, starved or suffocated in one of his own booby traps and gnawed by rats. Some 120 tons of junk was removed from the house.

Then there was Weegee, another familiar of the fringes. He was a photographer of genius, real name Arthur Fellig, who had been born in Poland in 1899, came to Manhattan as a boy and started his career as a peripatetic taker of children's portraits on the Lower East Side, moonlighting as a violinist in silent movie theatres. By 1945 he had found his vocation as a portrayer of Manhattan's darker sides, and had struck up a special relationship with the police and fire departments. He claimed to have psychic premonitions about crimes and fires, which is why he called himself Weegee, a corruption of Ouija, and from his seventeen-dollar-a-month lodgings behind the downtown police headquarters he would cruise the streets in his elderly Chevrolet picking up emergency messages on his radio, and often in fact being the first person to reach the scene of crime or conflagration.

A stubby, portly man in a pin-striped suit, cigar invariably in his mouth, Weegee was a haunter of slums and backstreets, a voyeur of love, poverty, perversion and pathos. "I caught the New Yorkers with their masks off," he said of himself in retrospect, ". . . not afraid to Laugh, Cry or make Love," and in the pursuit of his art he became a New York celebrity. His 1945 book of pictures *Naked City* was turned into a famous film, but his response to success was pure Manhattan: "You're as good as your last picture. One day you're a hero, the next day you're a bum." An amateur photographer once took a picture of *him*, and sent him a copy. It shows him fast asleep on a bench in Washington Square, wearing a crumpled suit and a collarless shirt, head lolling, unshaven, probably snoring, for all the world like one of his own more destitute subjects.[1]

And finally, to end this interlude of caprice, here are glimpses into the lives of two more private Manhattan originals of 1945. In his elegant penthouse on the Upper East Side, so *Life* magazine tells us, Mr. Elliott E. Simpson lies between his sheets of a morning while his parrot Sally, in bed with him, sings in a soprano voice to the accompaniment of his butler on a trumpet. ("Polly," says the magazine, "is considered brighter than some people by Mr. Simpson, who likes her although she once bit him"). And in her rather smaller apartment on the Upper West Side Miss Delphine Binger assiduously attends to her collection of several hundred thousand goose, turkey and chicken wishbones, prime examples of which, boiled and polished, decorated with charms or ribbons, she likes to send to well-known people when they are ill, married or elected to the Presidency.

---

[1] After the success of *Naked City* Weegee abandoned the crime and fire round, and devoted himself to less urgent forms of social photography, sleeping all day, spending the night in clubs and cafes, or simply roaming the city. He died in 1968, and there is a collection of his work at the Museum of Modern Art.

Village Life

Many such perimeter people, like Joe Gould, had gravitated to Greenwich Village, the tumble of streets, this way and that, which lay to the west of Washington Square, spilling into Chelsea in the north, and having as its focus the Square itself at the foot of Fifth Avenue. The Village was thought by most New Yorkers to be very pretty—its streets so distinct from the mechanical pattern of the city, its dormered houses small and trim, sometimes with pleasant gardens. Not many Europeans, deposited there without explanation, would give it a second look. Its houses were mostly ordinary really, its streets were cramped rather than intimate, and even Washington Square itself, for all its green foliage, was nothing special by extra-Manhattan standards. Visitors were generally taken to see the private alley of former stables called Washington Mews, many of which were inhabited by famous people, but to alien eyes even they looked uninvitingly poky.

Old hands never tired of saying that Greenwich Village had been tamed. In the years of Depression and Prohibition it had proliferated with political activists, profoundly concerned writers and artists, rebels and originals. In 1945 it had become, they said, positively dull by contrast—"respectably bourgeois, for goodness' sake," wrote Eleanor. Early; "rather staid" thought the editors of the *Look Guide to New York*. The arrival of the IND subway, in 1940, had brought the Village more into the mainstream of Manhattan life; artists were no longer defiantly alienated from the community at large; radicals were quieter these days, and there were, for the moment, few Gertrude Steins, John Reeds or Edna St. Vincent Millays to give the district their own peculiar stamps.

But newcomers found it wild and marvellous still. To Americans from the interior it was a dream of liberty and unconvention, to Europeans it possessed an air of bohemia mostly lost in their own ravaged or war-straitened cities. It still *felt* separate from the rest of Manhattan, away down there where the grid of the city failed. It had old pockets of Italian settlement, but it was generally multi-ethnic, or un-ethnic, and its proximity to the Hudson River piers—one of the busiest ferry stations was at the end of Christopher Street—gave it a tang of Sailortown. If it was perhaps less colorfully outrageous than it had been, it was still the most generally easygoing part of town, where nonconformists of every kind, Trotskyists, homosexuals, atonal composers, sniffers of cocaine, could pursue their preferences without disapproval or interference. As the reporters Jack Lait and Lee Mortimer hopefully reported of Village social events, "drugs and depravities are prevalent at some of these purple parties, which often turn into unspeakable saturnalias within draped walls, in musk-heavy air. . . ."[1]

---

[1] *New York Confidential*, 1948.

In the Village you could browse without buying in all-night bookshops. You could eavesdrop on coteries of the intelligentsia arguing in cafes as they argued so brilliantly in the memoirs of the aged—Cafe San Remo on Macdougal Street, Cafe Reggio just down the road, were almost Viennese in their acceptance of one-cup, long-stay customers. You could eat from a dozen cuisines, even if prices were rather less bohemian than they had been, or recapture some of the old thrill of Prohibition at saloons that still pretended to be speakeasies.[1] At the White Horse pub on Hudson Street ("The Horse") you could mingle with poetical abstractionists, resting actors, about-to-become-novelists and seamen from the North River. At the Minetta Tavern on Macdougal Street you might well find yourself in the company of, or even paying for the drinks of, Mr. Gould, and at the shabby Earle Hotel you might encounter P. G. Wodehouse, who liked to stay there. Artists still hung their pictures on walls and fences all over the place. Practitioners of the Raven Poetry Circle, under their Head Raven, still sold their work to passers-by in Washington Square, though the epic poet Gildea preferred to recite his each evening at the Village Vanguard nightclub. e. e. cummings was eschewing capital letters in Patchin Place, as he had for twenty years, and the Provincetown Playhouse on Mac-

---

[1] One at least still does: the game is given away at Chumley's on Bedford Street only by the credit card stickers behind its barred and narrow windows.

dougal Street, one of the most famous little theatres in America, having introduced Eugene O'Neill to the world in the 1920s was looking for talent still.[1]

If the midtown set went slumming in Harlem, they often went strolling in Greenwich Village, preferably after dinner on summer evenings, when the community was in the full blast of its exhibitionism, debating furiously on park benches, sitting backwards on sidewalk cafe chairs, drawing instant portraits in charcoal, or just meandering itself, up and down the little streets, trying hard not to be taken for tourists.

Among the Bourgeoisie

Of the 600,000 dwellings in Manhattan, only rather more than six thousand were owner-occupied. The lucky people who had whole houses to themselves were scattered in enclaves around the island, and often lived delightfully. Down at Gramercy Park they lived like Londoners, in houses with cast-iron porches and pretty balconies around a private square, and a little further uptown, at Sniffen Court on East 36th Street, they lived in ten charmingly converted stables, facing each other

---

[1] cummings lived there until his death in 1962; the Provincetown Theatre presently found Edward Albee.

across a paved yard and guarded by iron horses' heads. On the Upper East Side people like Eleanor Roosevelt, Tallulah Bankhead, Gertrude Lawrence and John Gunther lived in the four nineteenth-century blocks called Treadwell Farm, preserved by covenant forever against "any establishment, business or occupation . . . which may be dangerous or offensive to the neighboring inhabitants." There were some extremely upper-crust private houses along the East River, and some on the Hudson too, while the residents of Pomander Walk, on the Upper West Side, occupied a double row of mock-Tudor houses, named after an English play produced on Broadway in 1911, and architecturally modelled upon its stage sets.

Most of Manhattan's resident householders, though, lived in the familiar brownstone kind, which had gone through a period of social and aesthetic disrepute, but was now becoming admired again. These buildings, which were made of a Triassic sandstone containing iron ore, generally had a long-windowed parlor or drawing room on the first floor, a dining room above the kitchen, and main bedrooms with dressing rooms. They were proper bourgeois houses in fact, built for the rising middle classes of the previous century—before the silk-stocking vote, politicians courted the brownstone vote. Some of them had been beautifully restored or developed: the nineteen brownstones of Turtle Bay Gardens, on the East Side between 48th and 49th Streets, had been remodelled to form a kind of Manhattan Palais Royale, facing inwards upon a delectable common garden, and were among the most desirable residences in the whole island.[1]

The modern middle classes far more often lived in privately-owned apartment houses. The very first building of this kind, the Stuyvesant Building, was still standing at 142 East 18th Street, downtown: erected in 1869, it was a dour old structure without elevators, but it had transformed the city with its descendants.[2] Later blocks were far more showy, and had far showier names, too—consequential names like Majestic or Embassy, patrician names like Chatsworth or Trianon, literary names like Kenilworth or the Kipling Arms, peculiarly religious names like St. Rita, St. Valier or St. Urban. Some specialized in famous occupants. The monumental Ansonia, on the Upper West Side, was blessed with such thick nineteenth-century walls that Chaliapin, Caruso, Tos-

---

[1] As they still are: their residents in 1985 include Katharine Hepburn, Stephen Sondheim and Julian Bach the great literary agent. The willow tree that stands in the central garden was immortalized by E. B. White, in the final paragraph of his *Here Is New York* (1949), as symbolizing the city in its "steady reaching for the sun."

[2] Dour enough to make it a suitable location, in 1948, for the film *Kiss of Death*, in which Richard Widmark pushed an old lady in a wheelchair down its stairwell, it was comfortable enough to ensure that in all its eighty-eight years, until its demolition in 1957, it never once had a vacancy. Mrs. Custer, widow of the Last Stand, lived there. The Jane's of the Manhattan apartment block is *Living It Up* (1984), a comprehensive register by Thomas E. Norton and Jerry E. Patterson.

canini and Stravinsky had all found well-insulated homes
in it. The immense turreted Dakota had seemed, when
it was built in 1884 on West 72nd Street, to be absolutely
in the middle of nowhere, but had attracted an illus-
trious clientele of writers, actors and artists ever since.[1]
By the 1940s Manhattan was a city of apartment houses
like no other in America, and its most luxurious blocks
were very luxurious indeed: River House on the East
River had its own yacht berths until Robert Moses built
the Franklin D. Roosevelt Drive between it and the
water, and offered its tenants an average of twelve rooms
and six baths. Ineffably superior doormen guarded the
entrances of such establishments, wearing epaulettes,
cockaded hats or long buttoned coats like Russian gen-
erals, peremptorily blowing whistles for cabs and opening doors with majestic courtesy for ladies with poodles.

Most dizzily ambitious of all was the development
called London Terrace, in Chelsea, a block of fourteen
buildings that contained 1600 apartments, and claimed
to be the biggest in the world. There were guided tours
of this phenomenon, and many out-of-towners took
them. They were shown the monument to Clement
Clarke Moore, whose estate once stood upon the site,

---

[1] As it still does; beside its main entrance John Lennon was
murdered in 1980. The Ansonia, now finding itself conveniently
near the Lincoln Center of the Performing Arts, is still highly
cacophonous too (and in the 1960s its cellar was the home of the
celebrated sex club called Plato's Retreat).

and whose poem "A Visit from St. Nicholas" (" 'Twas the Night Before Christmas") was annually recited there by some celebrity or other. They took the elevator down to Main Street, the block's private shopping mall, with hairdressers, upholsterers, electricians, carpenters, a bookshop, a flower shop, cooking, baby-sitting and dog-walking services. They wondered at the world's largest private switchboard, and Manhattan's largest private swimming pool, and the infants' center, and the Residents' Club, where members could be observed playing bridge, taking language lessons, or listening to lectures. At first the doormen at London Terrace had been dressed up as London policemen, were known as Bobbies and were summoned to their duties by bugle-call; by 1945 the sheen had worn off rather (the developers had gone bankrupt, as a matter of fact) but they still found a celebrity at Christmas to declaim that poem before the monument.

Most people, of course, were obliged to live in blocks far more humdrum, especially as there was a chronic shortage of apartments—there had been no building since 1943, and wartime rent controls had encouraged tenants to hang on to what they had.[1] Your average East Side block, where people of several social and economic

---

[1] They do to this day. A contemporary ethical question of the city, says Warren D. Leight in *The I Hate New York Handbook*, 1983, is: "Would you save a drowning man if you knew he had a two-bedroom rent-stabilized apartment?"

ranks were likely to be living, in one grade of apartment or another, offered no more than a roof garden, a laundry, a valet service, perhaps a provision store, and usually kept its tenants only for a year or two. And up on the West Side, in the 80s and 90s, the streets were lined with virtually identical, run-of-the-mill, lower-middle-class apartment blocks, with no fancy names, just street numbers—each couple of blocks, in those days before supermarkets, having its own corner grocer, newsagent and saloon. Comfortable enough (elevators and steam heat), sufficiently respectable, inhabited by people of many races about halfway up the social scale, these were the kingdoms of the dumbwaiter—the shaft which, running communally through every apartment down to the service area in the basement, not only took care of garbage and deliveries, but intimately linked the apartments. Through the dumbwaiter you could hear your neighbours' quarrels, radios and piano practices; down it you could shout greetings or remonstrations, or ask for the loan of a vacuum cleaner. The dumbwaiter relieved the blandness of these somewhat impersonal dwellings, and perhaps gave to some of their residents twinges of nostalgia for the simpler life they had often left behind in the darker, more cramped, damper but sometimes friendlier tenements downtown.

Among the Poor

For the apartment block was only a development of the tenement, and if thousands of Manhattan families had graduated from one to the other, thousands more were living in tenements still—in Harlem, in the raddled streets of the Lower East Side, in the Gashouse district above 14th Street on the East River, in Hell's Kitchen, unexpectedly among the German gentilities of Yorkville, and indeed in splodges and enclaves almost everywhere on the island. Here and there one saw the rectilinear blocks of new city housing, courtesy of La Guardia, Moses and the New Deal; but for the most part Manhattan's poor lived extremely poorly still.

More than 71,000 Manhattan dwelling-places, in that prosperous year of victory, had no private lavatory. Some 3,500 had no running water. Some 20,000 people were living in cellars, it was said, and many more had no roofs at all, but spent their nights in Bryant Park, Union Square, and other well-recognized resorts of the homeless. The New York Foundling Hospital on East 68th Street took in at least 1,000 babies a year, most of them left inside the hospital by desperate young mothers.[1]

The tenements could be terrible. The most unspeak-

---

[1] Almost none are left there now, but this admirable hospital is still actively caring for children, supported partly by public, partly by private funds—tax, as the saying is, deductible.

able of them, of which a few were left, dated from the time when there were no building regulations at all, and unscrupulous agents and landlords could pack the maximum number of tenants into the most minimal accommodation—"lung blocks," they called them, because of their fearful incidence of tuberculosis. Many more were Old Law tenements, from the days when the law required only that a tenement should have an air shaft in the middle, and these were quite frightful enough; lavatories were shared, one to each floor, and inside rooms generally had no proper windows, only ventilators opening into the dark, narrow and foetid central air shaft, its walls stained with droppings, its inaccessible floor deep with garbage. The most diligent housewife could hardly maintain a decent home in a place like this. Damp got into everything, you could keep nothing clean, roaches were inescapable and rats brown, black and Alexandrian defied extermination— the only cure for rats, it was said, was to "build them out."

The survival of these cruel old structures, with all the crime, disease and unhappiness they fostered, was the worst of all indictments of Manhattan, at this happiest moment of its history. It was an indictment too of the ideology which had made the city in all its verve and splendour, for the tenements were without exception the product of private enterprise. The entrepreneurial zeal that would soon be going into the building of plush apartments for the well-to-do had gone, in previous generations, into the exploitation of simple immigrants, and had given The Landlord a name excoriated more vehemently in Manhattan, perhaps, than anywhere else. "If the roof caves in and the tenants are sitting in the debris," wrote Harry Golden, born and raised on the Lower East Side, "they will laugh like hell. They will endure any hardship as long as it means trouble for the landlord."[1]

And yet, and yet . . . the slums of New York were disgraceful slums, but there was no denying that they were interesting. They were among the most interesting slums on earth, and among the liveliest. Whether they were black slums, Puerto Rican slums, Jewish slums, they burst with vivacity. They were bursting with noise—shouts, hammerings, high-pitched squabbles, laughs, songs, swearings, radio music (they might have no lavatories, but 94 percent of Manhattan homes possessed a radio). They were bursting with things, from radio aerials and rooftop pigeon coops to the inevitable laundry lines, sometimes on sticks out of windows, sometimes trailing across streets. They were bursting most of all with people, especially in the hot weather, when there were people hanging from every window, people flat on the roofs, people sitting in pairs all down the diagonal fire ladders, people lounging on front steps, leaning against railings, sitting on the kerb or hilariously hos-

---

[1] Again from *Only in America*, 1958. By then Mr. Golden had left New York and was publishing his celebrated newspaper *Carolina Israelite*, written entirely by himself, in Charlotte N.C., where he described himself as being as happy as a mouse in a cookie jar.

ing themselves, if young enough, from the corner fire hydrant—hardly a book of photographs of Manhattan in the 1940s is complete without its statutory hydrant children.

Only the rock-bottom drunks and dropouts of the Bowery, the street of flop-houses in the shadow of the El, seemed to have lost all heart. There was no life left in these poor derelicts. Women safely picked their way across their recumbent forms, as they lay with their bottles on the sidewalk, and the police left them alone.

All an Elite

Did these astonishing contrasts of style and fortune make for social unrest? Apparently not much, except among the more aware of Harlem's blacks, for these were slums still bursting with hope, too. People did not feel themselves inextricably sunk in poverty. There was always the hope of getting out of the tenement, overtaking the landlord himself one day and moving into somewhere portered, roof-gardened, pooled and valeted in the East 60s. Before the war the Communist party had been strong in Manhattan, social protest had been articulate and there had been sporadic riots (one of them put down with particular ferocity by Police Commissioner Grover Whalen). But the war had brought new prosperity to nearly everyone. The edge was off radicalism.

La Guardia's policies had been generally conciliatory, and despite a spate of strikes the city was in mellow mood. The Black Nationalists had yet to formulate their passions in Harlem; some of the most active Communists had left the country for eastern Europe.[1]

Manhattan in 1945 does not seem to have been an envious city. Perhaps the best-known of all Weegee's photographs, entitled "The Critic," showed a pair of stupefyingly grand dowagers arriving for a performance of *La Traviata* at the Metropolitan Opera House. They would be sagging with the weight of their multitudinous diamond bracelets, necklaces, earrings and tiaras, were it not for their stately bearing. Beside them the 1940s equivalent of a bag lady, in an unbuttoned old overcoat and a shapeless velvet hat, clutches a shopping bag and stares at their corsages with furrowed brow and open mouth, as though she is saying something. It is a perfect image of Have and Have Not, yet there seems no malice or embarrassment to the scene. The dowagers sail gloriously past the camera towards their box (south side, no doubt), one with a smile of condescension, the other with a sterner mien: the bag lady looks as though she does not resent their superbia exactly, but is just deploring the taste of their jewelry, or perhaps declaring it fake.

Foreign visitors in fact were struck by the sense of

---

[1] Several had gone on the Polish liner *Batory*, sailing on the evening tide, which gave rise to a headline famous among newspapermen: REDS SAIL IN THE SUNSET.

comradeship which, especially in moments of particular amusement, relief or difficulty, bound New Yorkers together in those days. On winter mornings the hoisted red ball announcing that ponds were fit for skating brought people of all classes sociably into Central Park. Conversely a mute acceptance of shared suffering wryly united commuters in the morning rush hour. When blizzards howled through Manhattan, piling its streets with snow, or when a heat wave left the whole city gasping and sweating, a powerful fellowship blunted the edge of the common misery, bridging the most insuperable linguistic barriers, or the most unclimbable social barricades, if only with a wink or a grimace. In some ways New York was a familial community still. Its divorce rate was the lowest of any big American city. Only one in fifteen of its citizens had ever been to a nightclub, so the editors of the *Look* guide reported, and 92 percent were in bed by 10:30 p.m.

And anyway citizenship of this city in itself made for a bond beyond class. To be a citizen of Manhattan was an achievement in itself—it had taken guts and enterprise, if not on your own part, at least on your forebears'. The pressures of the place, its competition, its pace, its hazards, even the fun of it, demanded special qualities of its people, and gave them a particular affinity one with another. They were all an elite!

5

On Movement

CLANG! The concertina gate is opened, by a brawny boatman with his sleeves rolled up. There is a jangle of iron pawls, a creaking of planks. A slurp of muddy water, rich with cigar butts, old newspapers, bottles and oil slicks, rises and falls against the wooden timbers, and off the grimy ferryboat, with its tall black-belching funnel, the commuters from New Jersey fairly politely elbow their way along the pier, through the grim terminal at the bottom of 42nd Street, to fan out among the shops and offices of midtown. They are the descendants of the original commuters, the very word being a New York derivation from a commutation ticket—what the English still call a season ticket.

And they are only two or three hundred out of several hundred thousand. Manhattan was the ultimate commutation center, because nearly half as many people travelled to work in this island each day as slept in it each night. They travelled in fleets of cars, armadas of ferryboats, endless processions of trains, buses, streetcars, speedboats, by seaplane to one of Manhattan's four seaplane bases and even, over the boardwalks of the East River bridges, reverberating to the traffic beneath them as morning came up over the city, resolutely on foot. Twenty bridges, eighteen tunnels, seventeen scheduled ferries served this stupendous daily migration, and it was like no other work-progress in the world—for what other great metropolis was squeezed hugger-mugger like this into a few square miles of island?

Hostile observers likened it, naturally, to a daily run of lemmings, out of rather than into the water, and considered it the very negation of civilized urban arrangement: Frank Lloyd Wright for instance, who thought cities should be small, self-contained and in the middle of the countryside. To others the twice-daily spectacle of the commuters was part of the Manhattan excitement—the regular inflow and outflow, like a giant lung at work, the twin symbolisms of magnetism and rejection, the tide analogy, the sense of mighty absorption—like gravy soaked up by dry bread, as the writer Felix Reisenberg had pictured it in a rich simile.[1]

---

[1] Again from *Portrait of New York*, which also included the fine hyperbole: "Even if you went to the last lone planet, whirling about the final sun, you would often think of this Imperial City."

Movement was the essence of Manhattan. It had always been so, and now its sense of flow, energy and openness, elasticity as Charles Dickens had called it, was headier than ever. Half this city's skills and aspirations seemed to go into the propagation of motion.

The Railway Age

Manhattan stood on the brink of the Air Age. The airline terminal building on East 42nd Street, built in 1940 especially to serve LaGuardia Airport, was claimed to be the Largest and Most Modern in the World: from its basement buses left throughout the day to connect with the hourly flights to Boston, the eighteen flights a day to Washington, D.C., the twenty-two-hour flight to Alaska, the overnight flight to Mexico City, the flights, continued throughout the war, to South America and the Caribbean. But everyone realized that this was only the beginning. LaGuardia Airport was new—it had been built for the 1939 World's Fair—but since 1942 they had been at work on a far larger one beside Jamaica Bay in Queens. All the major airlines of the Western world were preparing themselves for services into New York, whether by land planes (Lockheed's Constellation was already being test-flown) or by flying boat, like the Pan-American services to Europe before the war—as Martin Aircraft confidently forecast in magazine advertisements of their huge new Mars flying boats, "They'll pay big dividends to tomorrow's airlines."[1]

Airline clerks, nevertheless, were still members of the Brotherhood of Railway Clerks. If the Air Age was dawning in Manhattan, the Railway Age was at its glorious zenith. Two million passengers flew into New York in 1945, but 70 million, all commuters apart, came by train.[2] In their several headquarters in the Transportation Building, 500 Fifth Avenue, the railroad companies were apparently permanently installed, each grander than the next, with their crests and entwined initials and silver-plated glass-cased model locomotives beneath oil-paintings of immensely whiskered late tycoons.[3] Long-distance rail travel out of Manhattan, far from fading out, was fast returning to its old efficiency after the vagaries of war. That meant unequalled con-

---

[1] But when the time came, tomorrow's airlines spurned the flying boat altogether—by 1946 seven airlines were flying from New York to Europe, and they all used land planes. The 42nd Street airline terminal was on the site of the present Philip Morris headquarters, and has never been satisfactorily replaced. Within twenty years the Jamaica Bay airport, now John F. Kennedy International Airport, was to be as large as the whole of Manhattan south of 34th Street (says the *A.I.A. Guide to New York City*, by Norval White and Elliot Willensky, 1967).

[2] According to *New York City*, by the editors of *Look*, 1948.

[3] The building is not so transportational now, but it does still house the offices of Polish Airlines, Valef Yachts of Greece Inc., and Airship International Ltd.

venience for the passenger. You could buy your ticket
at a hotel or a store if you liked; you could have one of
the express companies collect your baggage a couple of
hours before departure, to be delivered direct to your
train; when you stepped from your cab at the station a
redcap porter would be there to guide you to your
track, see to your hand baggage and pass you into the
care of your car conductor—who, standing at the car
door with his peaked cap and his clipboard, seemed to
be waiting only to check you in. No railroads in Europe
or Asia could match the great American systems, when
it came to customer service.

Two of Manhattan's greatest shrines, more preten-
tious than any of its churches or synagogues, beating
even the skyscrapers perhaps for monumental self-
importance, were the two railway terminals, Pennsylvania Station and Grand Central. Together they received
all the surface trains entering the island (though some
trains from New England went clean through Penn
Station, as everyone called it, by way of tunnels to the
New Jersey shore, giving rise to the witticism that Manhattan was no more than a stop on the Boston to Washington line).[1] Arriving at either of these destinations out
of the American hinterland was a moment of majestic

---

[1] And to the curiosity that on westbound through trains of the
Pennsylvania Railroad you couldn't get a drink until you were
halfway under the Hudson River—they had liquor licences for
New Jersey, but not for New York.

finality. Aesthetically Penn Station was perhaps the more admired, at least by architectural critics, and was a good deal busier, besides being the place (Track 29) from which the Chattanooga Choo Choo departed in a famous song of the time; but in the public mind at least, Grand Central seems to have been at once the more homey and the more prodigious, so that's the one we will visit.

There was no mistaking it. Midtown Park Avenue, in those days, consisted mostly of middle-height apartment blocks, one after the other down the wide double highway which covered the New York Central and the New Haven railroad tracks. It was one of the few midtown stretches of street of more or less even height. At 42nd Street however its way was brutally barred by a towered hump of buildings, built athwart the avenue, with tunnels to let the traffic through and a portentous group of hotels in attendance. This was the Grand Central complex. The tower was the headquarters of the New York Central Railroad, and the hotels—the Waldorf-Astoria, the Biltmore, the Commodore—had all been built by courtesy of the company, in its leased air rights, over its subterranean tracks.

The official address of the station itself was 89 East 42nd Street: the number was emblazoned in gold lettering at its main doorway. It was a massive neo-classical building south of the office tower, and its epicenter was the bulbous golden clock above the information desk in the Grand Concourse. If there was one meeting-place in Manhattan that would confuse nobody, this was it. Everyone knew it. Everyone had wondered at the vast pillared hall with its ranks of ticket booths, maintained almost sacerdotally, with not an advertisement in sight and a troop of fifty-nine cleaners to polish its floor in the early hours of each morning. Everyone knew—it had entered the folklore—that the picture of the zodiac on the high ceiling had something wrong with it: either Orion was back to front, or the Zodiacal belt itself was inside-out. Everyone had met someone, some time or other, at the clock in the Grand Concourse: 180,000 people caught or left a Grand Central train on an average day, so the railroad publicity men calculated, but 370,000 just used the station as a meeting-place, a shopping place, a hanging-around place or a short cut.

They would never see a train, nor even hear a whistle, for at Grand Central trains were kept severely in their place. You could easily spend a day there without suspecting the presence of the tracks. You could eat in the celebrated Oyster Bar, or go to the movies, or visit the well-respected art gallery, or listen to a recital on the electric organ in the Concourse. If you knew the trick you could enjoy yourselves exchanging frivolities in some of the lower level arches, which formed a kind of whispering gallery popular among college students. If you were ill you could go to the station hospital—on to the morgue if necessary. If you had introductions you could take a look at the brand new CBS TV studios, gearing themselves up for public transmissions very soon on the first floor of the station. If you were better-connected still you could call on Mr. and Mrs. John W. Campbell: they maintained a private suite there with a gallery, a pipe organ and a glorious collection of rugs. And if you had seen enough of the terminal itself, you could explore the subterranean network of passages connecting it with hotels and office buildings round about.

But if you were a train buff, of course, you would want to see the trains, and particularly the pride of the New York Central, the Twentieth Century Limited, which left on its 961-mile, sixteen-hour journey to Chicago at 6 p.m. each evening—or rather at 6:01, for it was the custom of this station to dispatch its trains a minute after the scheduled time. Trains entered and left Grand Central on two levels, the hundreds of commuter trains on the lower level, on the level above, the long-distance trains or "liners"—the Fast Mail, the Lake Shore Limited, the Detroiter, the Pacemaker, the Owl night train to Boston. All were hidden almost hermetically behind bronze doors, set in marble, which gave no idea of the gleaming stainless steel coaches, the bustle and the noise enlivening the gloomy tunnels behind. The Twentieth Century left from Track 34, and there was no mistaking its gate, for every night it welcomed its passengers along a grey and red carpet, with its own name woven into it, spread down a platform which, alone among all those at Grand Central, was known as "the quay."

The train had begun its career in 1902, with three

Pullman sleepers, a buffet and a diner.[1] By 1945 it ran six or seven sections of twelve cars each, with bunk dormitories next to the locomotives for the crews, including secretaries and valets. Over at Penn Station, at almost the same time each evening, the Pennsylvania Railroad's rival Broadway Limited also left for Chicago: but it somehow lacked the Twentieth Century's glamor—its name was not so resonant, and it took the southern route, over the Allegheny hills, instead of the heroic northern way across the often snow-bound prairies.

Almost six o'clock, and there stands the Twentieth Century now, its cars silver, grey and white in the half light, its observation car all glassy at the back. Its last passengers are hurrying to join it, its redcaps are wheeling their trollies away, its courtly conductors stand by their doors, and one or two press photographers, without a doubt, are flashing their bulbs at the miscellaneous celebrities leaving that night for Chicago—could that be Myrna Loy? Say, doesn't that look like Joe DiMaggio? Oh boy!

There is just time to take a look aboard, and we must snatch it, for this is one of the sights of Manhattan. The train has been styled throughout, inside and out, by the designer Henry Dreyfuss (he has even modelled the streamlined 4-6-4 Hudson steam engine which is waiting

---

[1] John W. Gates, a magnate of the time, was among the passengers on its initial run. In New York he told reporters that the advent of the train made Chicago a suburb of New York; at Chicago he put it the other way round.

to pick up the train out at the Harmon junction). It is all functional elegance—Dreyfuss himself calls it "clean-lined." Smooth, quiet, subdued, with hidden lights and restrained decoration of chrome, mirrors and photographic murals, it has nothing fussy or drawing-roomy about it, like the old Pullmans that it replaced. Venetian blinds shade the big windows, neon strips illuminate the dining room, electric eyes open the doors for us. Lucius Beebe, the most famous of all railroad enthusiast, thinks it "antiseptic."[1] Perhaps it is a bit clinical, but as the passengers board it now, the chrome and steel spaces are filled with life and warmth, the air-conditioners hum, the waiters hasten through the dining room checking place-layings, the conductors make a final check of their rosters and the last porter, tipping his hat and pocketing his doubtless handsome tip, disappears through the platform door (through which we can see, intermittently, the jostling heads of the admiring evening crowd, gazing in the general direction of Myrna Loy)— as the great train prepares for its departure it is a scene of beauty, the restlessness against the order, the swagger against the steel, the excitement of travel beside the calm assurance of the machine. "All a-*board*!" cries the loud-hailer in that romantic rising cadence beloved of the American train crier, "All a-*board* the Twentieth Century Limited, non-stop to

---

[1] He told me so, when having taken the Twentieth Century west during my first week in America, I called upon him at his home in Virginia City, Nevada. He lent me his Rolls-Royce, too.

Chi-ca-go!"—and in a moment, as we make a run for it, and the last umbilical cables are disconnected deftly from the observation car, the red rear lights of the train are disappearing down the dark tunnel beneath Park Avenue.[1]

Under the Streets

Heaven knows this was by no means a typical train departure out of Manhattan. Three railroads possessed land approaches to the city: the nine others serving it got no further than the New Jersey shore, and to catch their trains you had first to make your own way across the Hudson River on a railroad ferry—only the Baltimore and Ohio provided bus service from its Columbus

---

[1] The Twentieth Century Limited no longer runs, but it was the star of the Broadway musical *On the Twentieth Century* in 1978—redcaps tap-danced to the melody of "Life Is Like a Train," and at the second act climax a full-sized replica of a Dreyfuss 4-6-4 appeared for twenty seconds on the stage. The enormous Pan Am Building now dwarfs the New York Central tower, but the station itself seems to me much the same, except for the advertisements that now dominate the Grand Concourse, and the conversion of some of the ticket counters into off-track betting booths. Penn Station was demolished in 1963, despite agonized conservationist protests, to make way for the new Madison Square Garden.

Circle offices to its station at Jersey City. Many of the commuter trains were notoriously grubby, crowded and unpunctual. Besides, for every passenger who left or arrived by surface train, at least ten travelled on the subway, whose principal claim to popularity was that its fare was only a nickel.

Lately amalgamated, all three lines of it, under city ownership, the subway was awful and astonishing in about equal measure. There were many people around who could remember when it began, in 1904: still extant indeed was the directors' car made for the opening of the first line, fitted out with a kitchenette and mono-grammed china, and used to give visiting grandees the run of the underground. Yet it already seemed as old as the hills, and the very initials of its names, IRT, BMT, IND, were part of the Manhattan music.[1] Hideous de-scriptions were written of rush hour in the subway, when people of all kinds, races and ages found them-selves, as nowhere else, in intimate physical proximity. Pickpockets worked the subways, girls had their bottoms pinched, stations were filthy and many of the trains were old and stuffy, having no air-conditioning. The work-ing of the system was as baffling to most visitors as an ancestral ritual, and it seemed to have given up trying to

---

[1] Though hardly anybody knew what they stood for: Interborough Rapid Transit, Brooklyn Manhattan Transit, Independent Sub-way (whose official name was City Subway System). There is another one now—PATH, and nobody knows what that means, either.

explain itself—the numbers and letters that incomprehensibly designated its trains had been left over from the three original companies. Yet by and large the subway was tolerantly regarded. Nothing too terrible was likely to happen to you down there, even in the middle of the night, and the competition to be "Miss Subways" was one of the town's better-known distractions—she was elected every eight months by passenger vote, and for three months her picture was displayed in every one of 6700 subway cars, resolutely smiling.[1] People with nowhere to go sometimes used the subway as a temporary home—a nickel would get you in, it was warm and dry, you could stay down there as long as you liked, ride where you wanted, and at its extremities you could get out on a beach somewhere, or in the countryside.

And of course the subway had its devoted enthusiasts, like everything else in Manhattan. For a subway freak the thrill of thrills was to travel in the leading car of a train, beside the shut-off driver's cab, looking through the front window into the dark tunnel ahead. Then what excitement, especially if you were in an express! Nothing seemed to go faster than a Lexington Avenue express, say, hurtling through the tunnels of Manhattan—shaking with the speed of it, leaning around the bends—headlong through the 23rd Street station, where the passengers stood pale and wan in the dim platform light—magnificently over the intersection when the

---

[1] She was at once guyed and immortalized as "Miss Turnstiles" in the musical *On the Town*, 1944.

Queens line came in—gloriously pounding, seventy miles per hour for sure when you checked your stop-watch, through the deep tube beneath the crowded teeming island, clean under the skyscrapers of midtown, under the park, under Harlem, and at last through the underwater tunnel out of Manhattan altogether.

On the Streets

Up above the busmen labored through the long exhausting day. To foreigners they rivalled those steam jets as phenomena of the Manhattan streets. No bus driver anywhere worked harder, smiled more seldom, suffered fools less gladly than a driver of Manhattan. He was shackled to his mechanisms. Not only must he drive the bus, an unforgiving process of jerky stops and short bursts of motion, but all day long he must stack the money which dripped, like coffee through a percolator, through the glass sorting-machine beside his driving-seat, besides giving change, opening and shutting the hydraulic doors, cursing soundlessly at cab drivers and responding to the tom-fool inquiries of out-of-towners. His body seemed to be in endless twitchy motion—his eyes constantly flickering to the driving-mirror, to the fiercely gesturing cop outside, to the coins beside him, to the latest idiot passenger asking where Fifth Avenue was; and so the long hours passed, from East River to

Hudson, from Harlem to Battery, the bus lurching, the engine revving, the change-machine whirring and tinkling, the cops shouting, the fire engines and ambulances howling, the taxis getting in the way, the inspector waiting with watch and notebook at the staging post, and the towers of Manhattan passing all unseen beyond the windscreen.

The buses added little to the allure of Manhattan, except perhaps the lumbering double-deckers they called Queen Marys, after our ship.[1] They were municipally-owned, charged five cents except on the Fifth Avenue route, where the fare was ten cents, and made little contribution to the character of the city—one could hardly imagine London without its big red buses, but remove the buses from Manhattan and aesthetically one would hardly notice. On the other hand the trolley or tram, in the Manhattan of 1945, was like a mobile museum piece, a fascinating relic of the cable cars, the horse-trollies and the drays.

You could still travel by trolley over much of the island. South-north lines ran from the downtown financial district up to Harlem, several crosstown services took passengers to the Hudson ferry piers and the East River bridges. The system, actually an amalgam of several ancient lines, was called collectively the Third Avenue Railway System, and big letters on the front of each car identified its route, B for Broadway for in-

---

[1] Which lumbered their last in 1953.

stance, X for crosstown, W for Willis Avenue in the Bronx. This made it an altogether more promising proposition for the stranger than the gnomic subway.

The cars were varied, and piquantly enriched the street scenes of the city. There was a well-known exotic, Car 555, whose aluminum was never painted, giving it an albino look welcomed with joy by trolley-spotters. There were specialist vehicles of primitive presence—knobbly ungainly vehicles like rail-grinders, dump cars, snow-sweepers or slot-scrapers. Car number 10, a sand-sweeper, had begun life as a horse car, and many other old stalwarts were soldiering on, to the end of the line, after half a century of service—some of them, called "convertibles," had removable side panels which in fine weather allowed their passengers to ride just as they had in Edwardian toast-rack omnibuses. Some cars were worked by overhead lines, switched at termini in the time-honored way; others were powered by conduits or third rails in the ground; when a streetcar stopped for the convenience of its passengers, all other vehicles had to stop at least eight feet behind.

They moved ponderously. It took an hour and forty minutes to travel the length of the longest Manhattan route, from Amsterdam Avenue in Harlem to City Hall in lower Manhattan, and almost no passengers travelled the whole way. The streetcars were primarily local vehicles, neighbourhood, street-corner vehicles, and perhaps this made them all the more beloved—the trip down a couple of blocks to do the shopping, the school run, the ride to the subway station or the ferry: these were the purposes of the trolley cars, and made them feel companionable.

They were doomed. By the end of 1946 most street-cars carried numerical signs, besides those reassuring Bs and Xs, to tell people the numbers of the buses which would soon be taking over their routes; and within a few years the very last Manhattan trolley, the very last rail-grinder and slot-scraper, even Car 555 itself, had clanked its way into the cavernous car-barns of the Third Avenue Railway.[1]

Above the Streets

Above the streets ran the elevated railroad—the El as everyone called it, even in print, where it was spelt sometimes with a big E, sometimes a small. Once there had been five of these ungainly but enthralling systems on the island. Now only one remained, the Third Avenue El, which was run by the city, and whose four-car electric trains travelled on high metal girders from one end of the island to the other. The El's attractions were fast becoming less practical than archaeological—

---

[1] Though not necessarily into oblivion: the service ended in August 1948, but some of the less antique Manhattan trolleys were shipped in 1949 to Vienna, where for years they were to be seen trundling with revived aplomb around the Ringstrasse.

though its lease was not due to expire until the year 2878, it was already sentenced to be phased out by 1960. Its quaintly bobbled and bargeboarded stations were like something out of British India, with protruding windows and fancy balustrades of wood and iron. Steep covered staircases approached them from the streets below, and connoisseurs of the urban antique particularly cherished their shabby old waiting rooms, which had pot-bellied stoves in them, hurricane lamps for emergencies, and sometimes stained glass windows. Tourists found it fun to travel high up there above the street traffic, looking into third-floor windows and remembering when King Kong had torn bits of the El's track up, and thrown some of its cars about; amateurs of the system particularly relished the sinuous S-turn near the bottom of the run, where the creaking rolling-stock swung bravely through the downtown office blocks above Coenties Slip (there were few signals on the Third Avenue El, and the trains had very primitive brakes . . .). "Ride on the Open-Air Elevated," the Third Avenue Elevated Railroad's publicity bravely said, as its trains ploughed heavily through the rising exhaust fumes.

But the most interesting thing about the El was the particular sort of life that it engendered down below. Much of Third Avenue was cast in perpetual shadow by the presence of this mechanism, which kept real estate prices down but preserved for the thoroughfare the style of an earlier Manhattan. Great corporations and self-respecting department stores preferred not to be seen there, so the sidewalks were lined, even in mid-town, with small, unpretentious and sometimes shady shops, with family restaurants like the Original Joe's or Manny Wolf's, with racy saloons like the High Hat, Costello's or Clarke's, with cut-rate hairdressers and thrift shops and sellers of dog-eared girlie magazines, with the Beverly movie house that showed foreign films, with flop-houses and clip joints. It was a street that servicemen gravitated to, when they wanted to get drunk without too much expense, and it smelt of malt, and cigar smoke, and the varied vapors that were trapped within its cavities. Ever and again above it there sounded the rattle of ancient trains.[1]

Riding the Ferries

Doomed too was that 42nd Street ferry, like nearly all the ferries of Manhattan; and this was sadder still, for nothing was more absolutely New York than a ferryboat.

---

[1] These sensations are my own—the Third Avenue El was not demolished until 1955, when it took only six months to pull the whole thing down. The Avenue was immediately given new life, and apartment blocks erupted: but from their upper floors you may still sometimes make out where the stanchions of the railway stood, and if you are old enough imagine the picaresque sub-world that thrived in your youth down there.

The Manhattan ferries were nearly as old as the city itself, and sometimes looked it.

By 1945 most of them were railway ferries, linking the West Side of Manhattan with the various railway depots along the New Jersey shore, and their pompous but distinctly weather-beaten stations, down among the dock piers, were grandly emblazoned in the railroad manner, with huge clocks, flagstaffs, classical pilasters and enormous railroad names. There were hotels near the waterfront especially for passengers arriving out of the hinterland, but most of the ferry passengers were commuters, and for hundreds of thousands of Manhattan workers the twice-daily ferryboat trip was part of life itself, and a pleasant enough pause for the most part between train and office, office and train. The boat was crowded perhaps, but there were probably old acquaintances aboard, and there would be the freshness of the sea wind to enliven you, and the busy harbor scene around, and perhaps one of the great ocean liners coming upstream to her moorings out of the mist. There was a camaraderie to the ferryboats, and their mingled smells of grease, smoke, wet wood and sea wind remained in many an old New Yorker's memory when he had retired to die in Florida or California.

Every photograph of Manhattan's waterfront showed a steam-ferry or two. Their shape was unmistakable, for they looked a little like Mississippi riverboats, and a little like floating potting-sheds. They were ferryboats *in excelsis*. Identical at bow and stern, a shape foreseen by the local steamship pioneer Robert Fulton as long before as 1812, they had bulbous rounded ends, sat low in the water especially during rush hours, and were comfortably beamy. High on their superstructures their twin wheelhouses, one at each end, often looked rather like pagodas or gazebos, and their helmsmen could be seen through the windows grasping gigantic wooden wheels, like Mark Twains. High above all rose the tall and spindly black funnels—two funnels, sometimes— which gave the craft their prim and lofty stance (so lofty that soldiers embarking on them from the troop trains had sometimes assumed them to be their transports for Europe).

Like the trolleys, some of the ferry-steamers were immensely old. They had reciprocating steam engines, and their deck-covers were supported by wooden pillars, with carved neo-classical mouldings. Their staircases were of mahogany, and were supplied with spittoons. They belched a lot of smoke into the already opaque atmosphere of the harbor. It was obvious to almost everyone that they would not be sailing much longer across the Hudson River, now burrowed under not only by railroad tracks, but by road tunnels too, and by the autumn of 1945 every blast of the ferry hooter had a dying ring. There was however one bold, swift and handsome exception to this melancholy rule—the Staten Island ferry, with its double-arched station at Whitehall Street in lower Manhattan, its nine big car-and-passenger ships, and its thirty-six duty captains.

No bridge, no tunnel connected Staten Island with Manhattan, and by land it was nearly twenty miles from its still bucolic borough town, St. George, round the New Jersey shore and through the Holland Tunnel to the Lower West Side. Although for generations people had talked of bridging the Narrows, the entrance to New York harbor, and thus linking the island directly with Brooklyn and Manhattan, nobody had ever actually begun work—had never indeed built a bridge, anywhere in the world, long enough. So the ships of the Staten Island ferry were certainly not forlorn. On the contrary, they were as proud and spanking as ships could easily be, and were run with style by the city's Marine and Aviation Department, which painted its own title vastly on their hulls. They were some of the biggest ferry-steamers in the world, and as they steamed across the harbor at their habitual fifteen knots, were not in the least discountenanced by the towering Atlantic liners they encountered on the way, or the warships steaming up-river to the Brooklyn navy yard.

They ran all day and all night, every day of the year. They never turned round from one year to the next, their crews speaking always of the Manhattan end of a ship as "ahead," the Staten Island end as "astern." They were almost never empty, and their twenty-minute nickel ride across the harbor, with its incomparable view of the Manhattan skyline from the sea, had long since become one of the great tourist experiences of the city. As the poor old railroad ferries tacitly prepared themselves for the breakers' yards, the Staten Island boats sailed on as though they would never stop.[1]

"Like I Say . . ."

Often enough writers celebrated the ferries and the El; but surely a book was never written about New York, fiction or non-fiction, without a mention of the Manhattan taxi-cab. Cab-men the world over have always been "characters," but the Manhattan cabbie was famous beyond all his peers because of his insatiable appetite for conversation.

His cab was rather an absurd machine: a clumsy

---

[1] Nor have they yet, even the building at last of the Verrazano Narrows bridge having failed to put them out of business: the modern ships are more imposing than ever, and even now the fare is only a quarter. Except for a Coast Guard ferry to Governor's Island, still run much in the old manner, all the other Manhattan ferries have sailed their last. In 1967 I happened to be on the final public crossing of the final Hudson River ferry (the boat was the *Elmira*, built 1905 and still afloat, as I write, at Perth Amboy, New Jersey). "You ride this boat regular?" an old man asked me as we ploughed through the night to the music of the Hoboken High School band. "Never before in my life," said I. "Well you don't say. Some people have it easy. I've had to ride this ferry forty years to make the last crossing. You come over and do it first time."

yellow-painted car, purpose-built by the Checker Company or De Soto, into whose squashy back seats passengers stumbled rather than reclined. He was unlikely to be its owner, since most of the city's 11,796 cabs belonged to one of three big companies; but he was no part-time amateur like so many of his successors, and had no ambitions, as they would so often have, to go on the stage or write novels.[1] If he was not always too well-informed about Manhattan addresses, there being no professional examination or for that matter instruction, he was immensely worldly-wise, priding himself on his insight into character and his inability to be surprised by anything.

It was his habitual pose in fact, notorious among travellers everywhere, exploited by every foreign correspondent, to be one of life's natural philosophers. Folk-wisdom flowed freely from the front seat into the back: "What I say is, if a guy ain't true to what he thinks, that guy ain't worth thinking about," or "Like I say, there's no use working your ass off if the meaning of life's just passing you by." About Manhattan itself the cab-driver would generalize all day, if not discouraged—how there was nowhere else like it in the world, how it was full of jerks and bums, how the garbage it threw away would feed all Europe for a year, how all the

---

[1] Though several cab-drivers did write books, notably James V. Maresca, whose memoir *My Flag Is Down*, published in 1948, was racy with anecdotes and enlivened by chapter headings such as "Help Me, You Big Dumb Lug," or "Mister, Get Wise to Yourself."

cops were crooked—"See that dumb Irishman eating there? You think he's *paying* for that spaghetti?"—how the place would grind to a halt one day, if they didn't do something about the traffic, how Manhattan was the place where there was nothing, *nothing*, money couldn't buy—"The city that never sleeps, that's what they call it, the city that never sleeps. You never heard that before?"

All this beguiled some strangers, bored others to tears and provoked a few into intemperate retorts—"All right bud," says the driver, assuming an affronted look, "so you heard it before, take it easy, if you don't want me to talk I won't talk, that's your privilege. . . ." Perceptive customers, though, saw beyond the persiflage to the truth about your generic Manhattan taxi-driver, namely that all his salt, bile and pawky sentiment generally added up to a romantic sense of wonder about the city to whose character he made so inescapable a contribution. As James V. Maresca was to write, "Who knows what may happen? It's good just to dream in New York City, even though you're only a cab-driver."

Likely To Succeed

But then *all* the movement of New York was romantic, for those susceptible to civic history. This was a conduit, through which for nearly three centuries a never-ceasing flow of people and ideas had passed. In the 1920s the best place to catch a taste of this function had been Ellis Island: by 1945 its truest epitomes were perhaps to be found at the four long-distance coach stations, the Midtown Bus Terminal, the Dixie Bus Station, the American Bus Depot, the Greyhound Bus Terminal, which were all within a few blocks of each other near Times Square. The flood of foreign immigrants had momentarily subsided, but every year many Americans migrated out of the interior to this magnetic destination. From the segregated South came thousands and thousands of black people hoping for better things—refugees, almost; from everywhere else in America there came the continuing army of the ambitious, who knew that most of Manhattan's Big Shots, as the vernacular called them, had been born elsewhere.

The cheapest way to get to Manhattan was on a bus, so the arrival bays of the bus depots were the places to see the movement of Manhattan at its most metaphorical. They could offer poignant spectacles, of course: the noise and confusion of everything, as the heavy buses came and went in a scramble of diesel fumes, shouts, pushing and loudspeaker announcements, was enough to make the best-organized paterfamilias from South Carolina, the boy most likely to succeed at Leroy High, lose his cool just for a moment. These were great places for failing to find people, forgetting addresses, sitting on one's bags for a moment of tears and generally regretting that one had ever come.

But they were also places alive with eager astonishment. Black children's eyes were all agog, to see so much life, so much movement, so much money all around them. At the refreshment counter the pride of Leroy High ("Ambition: to be the best at everything") inspected with half-ashamed excitement the violently made-up and thrillingly short-skirted girls from 42nd Street climbing on to counter stools beside him. Lovers were reunited, prospective business partners shook hands, families from Missouri or Tennessee were whisked away to Harlem by friends who had come before: and hastening towards the exit and the waiting cabs we see the determined young secretary, soft-topped suitcase in hand, on her way to the Barbizon Hotel for Young Women, a job in a Wall Street stockbrokers' firm, and undoubted promotion, thirty years hence, to be the first woman vice-president of the corporation.[1]

---

[1] In 1950 these several bus depots were replaced by the Port Authority Bus Terminal, occupying two city blocks between Eighth and Ninth Avenues, handling 7500 buses every weekday, and suggesting to me, I see (in *The Great Port*, 1960), "something in Russia."

6

On Pleasure

Ten thirty. Jeepers! Just in time for the 10:32 into Penn. The thrill of it! Half last night we were practicing our swoons, till Mom came up and said it was time Gloria went home. We've waited months for this. Months? We sometimes think we've waited our whole lives. And today's the very day it's All Going to Happen! Oh, Glo, I don't know if I'm going to be able to stand it. Glo, what would you do if he actually *noticed* you? Could you survive, Glo? Wouldn't you just die there and then?

Wow, look at that crowd. Look at those cops. Boy, that's some crowd. That's Broadway for you. Think we'll make it, Glo? Sure we will. Push a bit, kick a bit, scream a bit maybe—there, see what I mean? Jeepers, what a place. D'you ever see such a place, Glo? Want some gum? D'ya bring the popcorn? Gee, Glo, I'm feeling kinda strange already. Think we can stand it, Glo? All these crazy girls, making like crazy? (Well, yeah, I know, but we're *us*.)

Oh hold me up, Glo, hold me up. The lights are dimming. Oh, Glo, gimme the popcorn, quick. Oh, oh, hear what they're playing, Glo? "Lovely Way to Spend an Evening"! Wow, look at those lights! Hear that beat! Oh that music! Hold me, Glo, don't let me faint, will ya, he's coming now—oh that horn, those lights, more popcorn, Glo—

FRANKIE FRANKIE BABY, I'M HERE!

Ah, those moments of *fin-de-guerre*, when the stars shone brighter than life from the great stages of the Broadway movie houses, and the bobby-soxers sometimes sat through all five performances, morning till midnight, and then stood in line again next day! No matter that it was All Happening for Gloria and her friend at 11:45 a.m., and that being well brought up, after baked beans and cherry pie at the Broadway Automat, or a soda at Schrafft's Spanish Garden under the Paramount, they would be home in New Jersey well before dark. For the rest of their lives their first memories of Manhattan in those postwar months would be memories of sheer pleasure. The city was equipped of course with all the usual apparatus of metropolitan delight, the marvellous museums and art galleries, the theatres and concert halls, but it had an extra element of entertainment, too, that was particular to itself: a special sting or buoyancy that enabled even the most sluggish pleasure-seekers, far less motivated than Gloria, to feel festive in the middle of the morning, or alternatively to stay up long, long beyond their bedtime.

These were celebratory times anyway, and in an era of big joyous musicals, jazz as general entertainment, pop music that at least did not alienate one age group from another, Broadway in particular epitomized the mood. A hit of the season was the musical *On the Town*, and there were some lines in one of its songs, by Betty Comden and Adolph Green, that could well stand as slogan to the time: "I could laugh out loud," the song exuberantly, magnificently cried, "I'm so happy to be me!"[1]

Razzmatazz

They were full-blooded times, too. Pick up a newspaper entertainment page for any day that year, and you will find it full of excess—stars with bellowing voices (Sophie

---

[1] The fact that teenagers of the day *practised* their swoons was recorded by Martha Weinmar Lear in the *New York Times* in 1974—she had done it herself.

Tucker, Ethel Merman), or huge generous mouths (Joe
E. Brown, Martha Raye) or prominent noses (Jimmy
Durante), or staring eyes (Jerry Colonna)—comedies of
uninhibited humor (Olsen and Johnsen in *Laffing Room
Only*, of which the *New Yorker* observed that "the boys
seem to be running out of ideas, not to mention taste")—
musicals with extravagant choruses and heart-on-sleeve ·
songs ("June Is Bustin' Out All Over," "New York,
New York (It's a Helluva Town)," "If I Loved You . . .").
When you went dancing you danced the whole hog,
jitterbugging and trucking to the blast of the saxo-
phones, now whirling, now stooping, now abruptly
precipitated by a change of tempo into a fox-trot cheek-
to-cheek. When you went to a club you were ready for
anything—bosom and blare at Billy Rose's Diamond
Horseshoe, America's Biggest, folk music at the Village
Vanguard, characterized by the *New Yorker* as being
hard to tell from a hole in the ground, the Hawaiian
Room at the Hotel Lexington where you drank out of
coconut shells, the Astor Roof where Harry James
played with his Music Makers nitely Sunday, the 23
Room at the Hotel George Washington where Dorothy
Ross sang her Frisqué Ballads, the Latin Quarter where
the food was limited to three All-American dishes (roast
beef, roast turkey, broiled steak), El Chico's where the
flamenco was first performed in Manhattan (people assumed it to be Jewish), the zebra-striped El Morocco
(people thought it was named for the Elevated Railway),
Club 18, "the Funny Place," where performers and
waiters were deliberately rude to customers (the Chinese

Ambassador was once given a bag of laundry), Sammy's down on the Bowery, where the poorest of the poor mingled with the richest of the rich, the Royal Roost (formerly Topsy's Chicken Coop) where the bop cultists stomped and clapped in their berets, dark glasses, goatees and string ties, the Parisian Room at the Plaza, where a featured performer that summer was "Walter Liberace, who plays piano to a victrola accompaniment."[1]

"Swing Street" was what they called West 52nd Street, between Fifth and Sixth Avenues, for in its hundred yards or so there flourished a dozen or more jazz clubs featuring some of the greatest performers of the day. These had started in the 1930s chiefly as resorts for jazz musicians themselves, after their evening gigs were done. They had been adopted by the Cafe Society, and had done much to project improvisational jazz as a popular art form, at a time when the regimented big bands were all-conquering. All kinds of jazz were played there cheek-by-jowl. At the Downbeat you might hear Charlie Parker and Dizzy Gillespie playing bop, bang next door at the Three Deuces Art Tatum was playing virtuoso swing, across the road Billie Holiday sang at the Onyx Club, immediately next door to the Onyx Dixieland and New Orleans jazz blared out from Jimmy Ryan's. Every sort of raffish and eccentric character mixed with

---

[1] Gone, all gone, except the irrepressible Vanguard, which having adapted to every change of taste and rhythm, in 1985 celebrated its fiftieth anniversary under the ownership of Max Gordon.

the swells in those smoky brownstone premises, and for many young New Yorkers they offered the best night out of all—you paid no entrance fee, you were charged no fancy Broadway prices, and over a single beer you could spend half the night listening to some of the best popular music in the world played live before your eyes.[1]

What else, on your evening out or your weekend furlough? A thousand movie houses, nine hundred more night clubs, a hundred burlesques surviving La Guardia's dictum that no navels must be shown on stage, a dozen dance halls where you could rent a partner at a dime a dance, Tony Pastor's Girlie Show, where you could inspect at your leisure the rather square-built if long-legged Pulchritudinous Damsels of the day.[2] If it was razzmatazz you wanted, Manhattan '45 was decidedly your place.[3]

---

[1] The clubs on 52nd Street, though an enamelled sign calls it Swing Street still, soon declined after 1945. Hoodlums and drug dealers infested them, and so many grubbier establishments moved into the street that it was nicknamed Sleazy-Second Street instead. Today most of the club brownstones have been torn down to make way for Rockefeller Center extensions.

[2] 5'4" was the minimum height for the Rockettes, the most famous of Manhattan chorus lines, 5'7" the maximum.

[3] Though Messrs. Lait and Mortimer (*New York Confidential*) thought the postwar crowds of servicemen and war-enriched civilians unworthy of its opportunities. "It takes many years of practice and some taste and intelligence to make a buck do the things New York can make it do."

To the Met

A glory of Manhattan was its theatre, unequalled in the world, at least at that particular moment, for variety, volume and in some respects accomplishment. Of the 680-odd so-called theatres in New York, about forty were still live theatres, some on and around Broadway, some in the first beginnings of the off-Broadway movement—the Yiddish theatres of the Lower East Side, the Provincetown in the Village. The greatest legitimate theatrical event of the 1944–45 season was the arrival on the Manhattan scene of Tennessee Williams, whose play *The Glass Menagerie* opened at the Playhouse Theatre. The *Times* was a little patronizing about it ("moments of rather flowery writing") but it was an instant popular success anyway, and made the thirty-four-year-old playwright, whose real name was Thomas Williams, instantly famous.

But Manhattan's mood in the summer of 1945 was essentially escapist, and the theatrical season was not, it must be said, otherwise very rich in serious art. It was dominated by comedies and above all by musicals, then being led into altogether new syndromes by Rodgers and Hammerstein's *Oklahoma!*.[1] The Broadway musical

---

[1] Which I first heard of when Noel Coward, entertaining the troops at the Stage Door Canteen in London, said he was going to sing something new and wonderful he had just brought back from New York: it was "The Surrey with the Fringe on Top."

truly orchestrated the time. Bertolt Brecht, then living in New York, said waspishly of it that it relied upon "popular stars, good scene designers, bad composers, witty if second-rate song writers, inspired costumiers, and truly modern dance directors," but he rightly saw it as "the authentic expression of all that is American."[1] That summer especially, when not only the seminal *Oklahoma!*, but *Carousel, On the Town,* and *Bloomer Girl* were all running simultaneously in Manhattan, the musical was reaching its fulfillment as one of the principal American art forms, and many a soldier disembarking from the *Queen Mary* that day would remember his passage through New York chiefly for one magical evening with the Broadway rhythms.

There was always plenty of classical music in Manhattan, too: at that moment it was certainly the greatest musical center in the world. A myriad chamber ensembles were in more or less constant performance, and there were four famous symphony orchestras in the city —the venerable Philharmonic, the City Symphony under Leopold Stokowski, the CBS Orchestra and the virtuoso NBC, founded in 1937 specifically for Toscanini.[2] Benny Goodman was blending American swing

---

[1] From his notes to *The Duchess of Malfi.* He added that it was an entirely phoney and empty kind of entertainment.

[2] It was disbanded in 1954 when Toscanini died, and today only the New York Philharmonic survives.

with European classicism—he had lately commissioned
a work from Béla Bartók (who died in New York that
year). All the great recitalists were lining up for their
postwar re-appearances at Carnegie Hall. And there
was always of course the Metropolitan Opera—the Met,
as all the world called it—one of the most utterly Manhattan of all Manhattan institutions.

Architecturally this was not among the world's most
seductive opera houses. It was an uncompelling square
building of dingy yellow brick, in neo-classical style, and
it stood on a part of Broadway, between West 39th and
40th Streets, that had once been the center of the theatrical scene, but was now in the middle of the garment
manufacturing quarter. It looked like a brewery, and
was extremely inefficient. Of its 3,778 seats, seven hundred were classified as "obstructed," or "side view,"
while backstage all was bare light bulbs, depressing
brown paint and tinny upright pianos. There was no
scenery store—stagehands had to work all night to move
the sets in and out for the next day's opera. Most of the
stage machinery had been unchanged since the 1890s,
and things frequently went wrong; it was at the Met that
Leo Slezak, waiting unavailingly for the swan to pick
him up in *Lohengrin*, inquired loudly "When does the
next swan come?"

The old place had glamor, all the same. At night
when the garment factories were closed, it alone blazed
with light down there, and the stage props so often to be

seen leaning against the outside walls, there being
nowhere else to put them, gave passers-by a thrill of
romance, as they glimpsed Roman dungeons or attic
walls of Montmartre propped there on the Seventh Avenue sidewalk. A first night at the Met was still a great
occasion, its comings and goings watched bemused by
the street crowds. The glitter of the Diamond Horseshoe, the gallery of thirty-five private boxes which had
its own segregated and grander elevators, was all one
could ask of operatic myth. Seats could be held by
hereditary right, some legatees being descendants of the
original subscribers in the 1880s, and an ineffable air of
satisfaction attended many of the box-holders, in particular, as they surveyed the scene before them through
their mother-of-pearl opera glasses, waiting not always
too impatiently for the curtain to rise.

The Met's artistic quality was thought by connoisseurs to be improving. Its manager, Edward Johnson,
was a jolly Canadian tenor (he used to launch into "Oh
What a Beautiful Morning" at moments of stress) whose
policy it was to introduce as many American singers as
possible: no blacks had yet appeared, but Johnson had
already introduced to the stage Dorothy Kirsten, Jan
Peerce, Richard Tucker and Robert Merrill. The music
critic Winthrop Sergeant, however, thought that art
hardly mattered to the Met's audiences. Most of its
patrons, he said in an article in *Life*, regarded opera
fundamentally as a branch of athletics—"They will

cheer a well-placed high F the way a baseball crowd cheers a magnificent back field run.''[1]

Eating Out

In Manhattan more than in most cities the pleasure of eating out often smacked of show business. This was partly because there was an old tradition of music in restaurants, from gypsy quartets to singing waiters (or for that matter singing customers, for several establishments encouraged diners to join in).[2] But it was chiefly because showmanship was considered a necessary part of the restaurateur's business. Irish restaurants in Manhattan were almost unnaturally Irish, Viennese restaurants oozed *Gemütlichkeit*, waiters in hunting pink were liable to serve diners at English eating places and there

---

[1] The Met was under sentence anyway. At least ten locations had been considered at one time or another for a successor, among them sites at Washington Square, Columbus Circle, 110th Street far uptown, Turtle Bay on the East Side and what was now Rockefeller Center. It was not however until 1966 that the present Metropolitan Opera House opened its doors at the Lincoln Center for the Performing Arts.

[2] Chinese restaurants unexpectedly specialized in jazz entertainment—Irving Berlin had begun his career as a singing waiter on Pell Street—and this practice was revived in the 1980s by the Chinese Tea Room on West 56th Street, over whose sweet-and-sour sounded the incongruous piano of Ellis Larkins.

were trattorias which depended almost entirely upon
the authenticity of the crone in black to be glimpsed,
like that Chinese postmistress's mother at her prayers,
backstage in the kitchen. At Mike's Ship-A-Hoy you
could eat in the wardroom of a mock-up submarine.
Keen's chophouse, which served two-pound mutton
chops with one-pound baked potatoes, was hung all
around with thousands and thousands of clay pipes.
Many visitors patronized the Automats as much for the
mechanism as for the food.[1]

Among Europeans eating out was not usually imagined as one of Manhattan's chief pleasures, but in those
days there was excellently down-to-earth American (and
immigrant) food to be found in many of the city's restaurants. At one end the fastidious Plaza offered boiled
salt mackerel, fried hominy grits, pecan waffle, clam
juice, little pig sausage and fried cornmeal mush. At the
other innumerable modest establishments served grand
old Jewish staples like bagels and lox with cream cheese,
hot pastrami with rye, pickled tomatoes and egg cream
(milk, chocolate syrup and seltzer). A three-course terra-
pin dinner served at the Century consisted of Robbins
Island oysters, buttered terrapins and canvasback duck

---

[1] Though local people sometimes went for the free soup which
you could concoct from tomato sauce, hot water and pepper—one
reason perhaps why Horn and Hardharts now operate under
franchise as Burger Kings, leaving only one Automat, on 42nd
Street, still automatic in Manhattan now. Mike's has put its last
customer ashore; Keen's is still ornamented with those pipes.

with wild rice—after which several members went on to a restaurant. The Sunday Strollers' Brunch at the Essex House, Central Park South, offered that summer prune juice, sauerkraut, fresh jumbo shrimps, cherrystone clams, a cereal called PEP, Scotch woodcock, patty of sweetbreads, creamed finnan haddie on toast, codfish cake with poached egg and tomato sauce.[1]

The city was rich in hearty, all-American restaurants, full of fun. It was fun to order one of Reuben's famous double-decker sandwiches, named after celebrities— "one Clark Gable coming up, one FDR with ketchup." It was fun to crack lobster claws at The King of the Sea or His Royal Family of Fish. It was fun to eat a steak dinner at Joe Madden's on West 56th, just off Fifth, whose menu said "If you enjoy your meal, we are glad and if you don't well go somewhere else." It was a joy to watch the women of Manhattan in their nice hats enjoying fudge pecan sundaes or apple pie à la mode at the fancier chain restaurants, Longchamps, Stouffers or Schrafft's—as the poet Phyllis McGinley wrote,

> Dear to my heart as to Midas, his coffers,
> Are the noontime tables at Schraffts and Stouffers . . . [2]

---

[1] I have the menu before me now. Ms. Mary Miller Freeman, who kept it after a visit to Essex House in May 1945, liked the Scotch woodcock but wrote at the bottom of the card "Lousy Service."

[2] She wrote it for a special supplement produced by the *New York Times*, in 1953, to mark the city's tercentenary. Reuben's, by the way, now offers Robert Redford, Barbara Walters and Mayor Koch sandwiches.

There were some truly exceptional tastes to be tasted, too, especially in seafoods. Nothing in the world could beat a soft-shelled crab from Chesapeake Bay, eaten preferably inside a crusty roll on a street corner downtown. Incomparable oyster stews were prepared at the Grand Central Oyster Bar by Viktor Yesenky and his thirty-six oystermen. Louis Massan's waterside restaurant on Fulton Street, beside the fish market, offered its customers (sitting at communal tables) five kinds of roe, tongue of cod, sturgeon's liver, squid stew and the cheeks of cod and salmon.

The trouble began with the dread word *gourmet*. It was odd but true that the bourgeoisie of Manhattan, the most cosmopolitan city in the world, knew very little about foreign food—the menu at Kirby Allen, a smart restaurant on Madison Avenue serving the carriage trade on cook's night off, included such items as "Lasagna, a Very Interesting Italian Dish."[1] Few diners-out took their food at all seriously, and the best-known food guide of the day, Lawton Mackall's *Knife and Fork in New York*, was not very urbane either—"eminently okey-dokey" was among its categories of commendation.

Many of the lusher "gourmet" restaurants took full advantage of this naïveté. They depended upon a heavily sauced and all too frequently flambée'd opulence of cuisine, supported by an unnerving tendency to talk in

---

[1] According to Mrs. Ariane Batterbury, a customer there in her youth, as quoted in the *New York Times Magazine*, November 1984.

French, and they charged outrageous prices—the Chambord on Third Avenue was said to be the most expensive restaurant on earth.[1] The tone of these places was set by the head waiters, who frequently expected enormous tips, and distributed good tables rather as a corrupt monarch might bestow largesse upon his toadies. It was said of the most famous of all maitres d'hôtel, Oscar Tschirky of the Waldorf, that "three generations of travelers and diners-out were flattered because their opulence, their social position or their public standing entitled them to call this former bus-boy Oscar."[2] The expense account had not yet entered its fulfillment in Manhattan; experienced head waiters could tell almost to a shrimp cocktail how much a customer was worth.

Yet even in the gourmet trade there were portents of better things to come. At 5 East 55th Street, just off Fifth Avenue, M. Henri Soulé from Paris ran Le Pavillon, a restaurant which had been started as part of the French pavilion at the 1939 World's Fair, and had moved into town when the fair ended. It was a restaurant in the grand French manner—Soulé, who was a

---

[1] It is now buried beneath the glassy substance of the Crystal Palace Pavilion. Some restaurants capitalized upon their expensiveness, but even in New York there were limits: *Less than that would they charge? More than that would they dare?*

[2] From his *Times* obituary in 1950. By 1945 he had retired from the Waldorf to his farm in upstate New York, but one of the hotel's restaurants is named after him still.

small fat man of autocratic tendencies and insufferable conceit, defined his own kind of meal as comprising mousse of sole, pilaff of mussels, pheasant with truffle sauce and meringue with custard and caramel, the whole washed down with vintage champagne. But unlike the Chambord and its kind, it was a restaurant seriously dedicated to good cooking. The food really was the thing here, and Le Pavillon was made famous by epicures of the less exhibitionist sort (J. Edgar Hoover of the FBI ate there regularly, encouraged by an unvarying bottle of Romanée Conti on the house).[1] Le Pavillon sounds ghastly enough, and all that champagne, all those truffles and meringues would hardly suit later Manhattan tastes, but it was the true beginning of la haute cuisine among the restaurants of the island. Within a few years European critics were to be calling it one of the best restaurants in the world, and it was to find imitators of varying distinction everywhere from Washington Square to, well, 65th Street, say.[2]

---

[1] He was left a watch—"To my dear friend"—when Soulé died.

[2] Le Pavillon moved in 1947 to East 57th Street (on its site now stands the First Women's Bank) and after training in its kitchens many of the chefs and restaurateurs who were presently to make Manhattan gastronomically supreme, is now long gone. Its original premises were taken over by another Soulé foundation, La Côte Basque, which still flourishes, and in which M. Soulé died of a heart attack in 1966.

Drinking

It would be wrong to deny drinking a section of its own among the city's pleasures. Manhattan loved its liquor— loved it all the more since the traumatic experience of Prohibition, repealed only twelve years before. Not only did every quarter, every block almost, have its own saloon, but many trades and callings had theirs too. Newspapermen hung out at Bleeck's, next door to the *Herald-Tribune* offices, artists at the Cedar Tavern on University Place. Writers favored the bar of the Algonquin Hotel or Costello's on Third Avenue. Seamen were at home in "The Horse." Advertising men frequented the intimate East Side piano bars (though their lyrics, in 1945, had mostly been silenced by an entertainment tax, penalizing vocalists but tolerating pianists on the alleged grounds that piano music was good for the digestion).[1]

Some of the saloons had changed very little since *before* Prohibition. McSorley's on East 7th Street was lit by gas lamps, had sawdust on the floor and declined to admit women, the only exception being a pedlar of peanuts called Mother French-Roasted; it served its ale in earthenware mugs, and many of its clients were Irishmen

---

[1] Explained to me by Mr. Johnny Andrews, who first sang and played at the Monkey Bar on East 54th Street in 1943, and who after war service as a bomber pilot survived that inquitous tax to be singing and playing there still—the same songs, too.

taking time off from doing nothing on the Bowery. And Clarke's in the shadow of the El, its bar-room darker even than the street outside, was where many a midtown businessman, at the end of a long day, wistfully postponed the journey home, besides being the ironic setting of the film *Lost Weekend*, that classic exposé of alcoholism.[1]

The drinks they drank were mostly beers, whiskies and cocktails, those elixirs and talismans of the 1930s. The Manhattan had been invented, so it was said, at the Manhattan Club, where they made it of one part vermouth, two parts whiskey, a dash of bitters, stirred with ice and garnished with a cherry; but it was the dry martini that had become to the world at large as emblematic of this city as beer was of Munich. Astonishing amounts of it were drunk, often so palely touched with vermouth that it was virtually pure gin, no less at mid-day than in the evening; many an ageing citizen of this city, in future and more health-conscious years, would look back wistfully to the long martini lunch hours of the 1940s. Wine was drunk far less, and mostly in ignorance. Heavy clarets and red burgundies were the dinner-party stand-

---

[1] Both are still doing fine. McSorley's, whose motto was "Good Ale, Raw Onions and No Ladies," had been made famous by John Sloan's painting *A Mug of Ale at McSorley's* (1913), and more recently by Joseph Mitchell, and apart from accepting women in 1970 it has never much altered its attitudes. Clarke's however found itself in new circumstances with the disappearance of the El, and in 1987 as P. J. Clarke's is one of the trendiest bars in town.

ards, whites being much less highly regarded and American wines seldom served at all. The subject of wine was often approached with childlike diffidence; even in the very fashionable Cotillion Room at the Pierre it said on the wine list (which included an 1887 Grand Chambertin): "We have been fortunate in having the help of a Grand Officer of the noble 'Confrerie des Chevaliers du Taste Vin,' who assures us that many of the wines are of the type one finds in the great cellars of Europe." There was only one serious retail wine merchant in the whole of Manhattan, unless you counted Schapiro's the kosher wine merchants of Rivington Street—the Sherry Wine and Spirits Co., Inc, on Madison Avenue at the corner of 61st Street, soon to be metamorphosed by amalgamation into Sherry-Lehmann, and to become one of the most famous wine firms in the world.

In 1945, when wine shipments were only just being resumed from Europe, Sherry's was still in its youth, having emerged like so many of its trade associates out of speakeasy days. It catered to a clientele more merry than pedantic, and had never acquired the solemnity thought proper to eminent wine merchants in Europe. Its window displays were colorful and breezy. Its catalogues were very jolly, and illustrated with comical cartoons ("Our senior executive watching our junior executive as she watches the keeper of our rarest Burgundies"). It offered a special Bon Voyage service for transatlantic liner passengers—"Your favorite Champagne is iced, packed in our distinctive buckets and delivered to the ship ready for opening and imbibing."

In short it was a kind of happy afterthought of the 1930s, and all the racy, raffish, heedless and disrespectful high spirits that Prohibition had paradoxically fostered. But by 1945 it was becoming far more too. Sherry's buyer Frank Schoonmaker was probably the best judge of wine in America, and under his influence the embryo wine-appreciation of New Yorkers was being assiduously fostered (and with it the mockery, arising out of an older tradition of American drinking, of people like James Thurber—"It's a naïve domestic Burgundy without any breeding, but I think you'll be amused by its presumption . . .")[1]

Al Fresco

New York was the sports center of the United States—nothing counted unless it happened in New York, and basketball and ice hockey only became national sports when they had found themselves Manhattan arenas. Madison Square Garden, an unobtrusive building on Eighth Avenue in midtown, was the chief of all American sports stadiums: to "fight in the Garden" was the

---

[1] Sam Aaron, now head of Sherry-Lehmann's, has succeeded Schoonmaker as perhaps America's best-known wine man, but I am glad to say his firm has still not subsided into gravity or pretension.

ambition of every boxer, and everything from rodeos and circuses to ski-jumping and dog shows happened there—during the annual six-day bicycle races, for which admission was one dollar, many vagrants took advantage of the occasion to move in for the week. Three of the top American baseball teams were more or less local: the home ground of the Dodgers was over the East River in Brooklyn, the Yankees were up in the Bronx, the Giants were based at the Polo Grounds in Harlem.[1] The classic outdoor pleasures of Manhattan, though, were nothing to do with organized sport, but reached back to simpler times, when just to be free, safe and preferably solvent on American soil was fulfillment in itself.

A steam-siren toots. A bell rings fussily. "Mind the gangplanks! Sailin' now for Bear Mountain, stops at Yonkers and Indian Point. All aboard for Bear Mountain excursion!" Jammed as they were in their narrow island, cooped up so often in narrow quarters, Manhattan people had always loved to exert their islanders' prerogative, and take a trip on the water. Steamboat rides had been available here almost since steamboats were invented, and there was scarcely a citizen of the town who had not enjoyed an excursion at one time or another. Among old people some of the brightest recollections of the Good Old Days were memories of outings

---

[1] The Dodgers and Giants have gone elsewhere now, and the Garden, reincarnated in 1968 on the site of the demolished Penn Station, is about to move yet again.

on the Manhattan pleasure boats: to Coney Island, along the New Jersey shore, around Long Island Sound or Upstate on the Hudson River.[1]

They were still sailing in 1945, to the same old destinations, in the same old style, and often in the identical old boats. Sailings were mostly from the Hudson River piers, and contemporary photographs generally show a pleasure boat or two moored among the freighters and the liners there. Even the look of them was festive, with their high straight prows, their tall and slender smokestacks, the awnings on their sun decks and the big freshly-laundered Stars and Stripes at their sterns. Pictures of their sailings look astonishingly anachronistic. It is hard to credit that this was the age of the jeep, the jet and the nuclear bomb, as one re-visits these quaint scenes of recreation. The ships themselves were often fascinating veterans. The *City of New York*, being driven by non-feathering paddle wheels made in 1912, not only made a peculiar plopping noise as she sailed along, but never did reach a speed in excess of ten knots, resulting in rather protracted pleasures. The side-wheeler *Robert Fulton*, built in 1909, was one of the most familiar sights of the whole Manhattan waterfront—people had grown up in the knowledge of her

---

[1] Though some also remembered the worst of pleasure boat tragedies, the fire on the paddle-steamer *General Slocum* which had killed 1,021 people in 1904; every year the Organization of *General Slocum* Survivors met at the cemetery in Queens where the victims were buried.

three black smokestacks, side by side, protruding above Pier 81, or on Sundays above Pier 1, beside the equally antique firehouse of Marine Company No. 1.

The passengers, hastening for the gangplanks in their cotton frocks, shirt-sleeves, white high-heeled shoes like Minnie Mouse's, look carefree and expectant. But thronged there upon the quayside they also have to them, as in mirror image, a little of the jostling pathos of the immigrants, while above them those who have already boarded sit on their deck chairs and benches with airs of undisguised complacency, as though they have long been assimilated. The captain leans for a moment languidly against the door of his wheelhouse, chatting to the mate inside; but a few moments later, when the ship has backed from the quay and is steaming away with snorts of steam and smoke, paddles clanking and streaming, colored all over with the whites and blues and fluttering scarves of its passengers, we may see him standing commandingly up there as though he is steaming them all to glory—confident in the knowledge that the *Clairmont,* even though she was built in 1911 for the night liner service between New York and Catskill, nevertheless amply complies with the safety regulations of the United States Coast Guard.

Manhattan's other allegorical escape into fresh air was a visit to Central Park, that vast pleasance, two and a half miles long by half a mile wide, twice as big as the Republic of Monaco, which had been dedicated from the beginning to the recreation of everybody. This was no Royal Park, like the parks of Europe, made available to the citizenry as grace or favor. This was the people's park *par excellence*, as populist as anything in Soviet Russia, and was for many residents of Manhattan the nearest they had to a garden. In 1945 Central Park was not quite as it had been when Frederick Law Olmsted and Calvert Vaux laid it out in 1857, Robert Moses having inserted playgrounds, tennis courts, ball fields, a zoo and the Tavern-on-the-Green restaurant near its southwestern corner: this occupied the former quarters of the park's resident flock of sheep, exiled to Brooklyn in 1934, and was attended by doormen in top hats and hunting coats, while an orchestra in forest green played upon its terraces. But at least Central Park remained, as its makers intended, a slab of open country in the middle of the great city. New Yorkers thought it intensely beautiful, and were very proud of it. Foreigners were not always so sure, finding its picturesqueness too contrived and its rocks of greyish basalt rather gloomy.[1] Everyone agreed though that on the right day it could provide much pleasure, and for most tourists it was outclassed only by the Empire State Building and Broadway as the prime attraction of the city.

During the Depression hundreds of squatters had put up their poor shacks in the park, living in cruel irony within sight of the Fifth Avenue and West Side apartment blocks, and frightening many respectable

---

[1] Twenty years later the English novelist Peter Ackroyd suggested that New York must have been built to afford some kind of relief from it.

burghers away; Collinson Owen, writing in 1929, had said that a man strolling in London's Hyde Park after nightfall might possibly find himself in a police court next morning, but a man who strolled in Central Park after dark would almost certainly find himself in the morgue. By 1945 the shanties of Hooverville were no more than a miserable tale, and if we are to believe the memoirs and the old photographs the park had been restored to a surprising sedateness. The old barouches plodded their way round and round the winding roads, filled with happy tourists or jolly conventioners, and driven in those days as often as not by well-dressed, sometimes top-hatted coachmen. People dressed apparently for church, office or social engagement sat decorously on benches around the boating pool, or watched the passing parade on the long Avenue. They played sportsmanlike baseball in Central Park, they flew kites, they threw horseshoes, they rowed boats, they skated in winter, on Sheep Meadow when the weather was right they played croquet.

At the top end of the park, where it impinged upon Harlem, one did observe pastimes of a racier kind, but for the most part Central Park in 1945 appears decidedly genteel. It was a place for family pleasures. No transistor radios blared upon the morning. No buskers twanged their guitars. No wild roller skaters careered around those bosky lanes. Even the jogger was a rare figure, and was generally assumed, if spotted, either to be training for the first postwar Olympic Games, or to be one of those New York eccentrics one had so often heard about. As for crime, police records tell us that in 1945 Central Park was one of the safest places in the whole of Manhattan, where almost nobody would have the heart to pick a pocket or grab a passing purse.

A Day Out

So let us ourselves, before we leave this world of pleasure, live it up for a day in Manhattan. Coming as we have from the other side of the ocean, the prospect before us is one of almost unimaginable delight, so astonishing is the contrast between this shimmering, bright, rich and wonderfully entertaining metropolis, and the grey shattered capitals of Europe.

We will stay at the Plaza, because if it is not the jazziest, or the most modern, or even the most expensive hotel in Manhattan, it is we are told the New Yorkiest. Just to wander through its salons after breakfast is an experience unique to New York: the smart page boys in their pillbox hats saluting us as we pass, the svelte and scented Americans, their clothes so *new*, their hair so exactly coiffed, smoking their cigarettes on squashy sofas in the lobby. The hefty doorman in his red coat tips his cockaded hat almost imperceptibly as we step into the sunshine of the square outside—and then the unmistakable light of Manhattan strikes us out of a pale sea-sky, throwing the tall shadows of the skyscrapers at

our feet. Ceaseless but orderly flows the traffic up and
down Fifth Avenue, the fat yellow cabs, the looming
double-deckers, the policeman urgently waving them
on at the 57th Street intersection. Insistently blow the
whistles of the doormen, far and near, calling for taxis.
A strong smell of horse-flesh and dung reaches us from
the barouches lined up over the way.

Sight-seeing first! Into the first and fortunately least
dowdy of these vehicles we step, and the driver turns out
to have been coachman—could it be true? "Sure it's
true, would I be putting you on, decent people like
you?"—to the Cornelius Vanderbilt IIs when they lived
on the corner there. The old mare snuffles and wheezes
a lot as she is prodded at an economical shamble around
the park, where two or three riders are exercising their
rather more athletic horses, and a solitary lady in blue
is setting up croquet hoops.

Down to Pier 83 next, in a taxi whose driver ex-
plains to us the true meaning of existentialism, besides
letting us into some surprising secrets about the Parks
Department, before he debouches us beside the gang-
plank of the yacht-like Circle Line steamer *Tourist*,
built 1906 (for which we are grateful—it might have
been the lumpish *Visitor* on duty, or the poor old
Islander, which looks like a duck). It takes three hours
for her diesel engines to propel us around Manhattan,
but we begrudge not a moment. Is this not the most
famous boat ride in the entire world, bar none? Do we
not pass under twenty bridges, including several that
are, so the captain assures us over his public address

system, the biggest, most beautiful, heaviest or busiest of their kind in the Western Hemisphere? Are we not offered some characteristic Manhattan pleasantries? ("Now I'm goin' to tell all you good people something strange about New York City. We call it the East River when it ain't no river, we call it the North River when it's in the South. No wonder you out-of-towners think we're crazy.")

A light lunch somewhere, don't you think? Something at Schrafft's? A bowl of Mr. Yesenky's oyster stew? Some of the Scotch woodcock Mrs. Freeman recommended during that interminable brunch at the Essex House? Then a brief run around the Metropolitan Museum (after all, we're not *entire* Philistines), and an hour or two at the shops. Altman's first, because they say it is the last of the really old-school stores, still down at the corner of 34th Street when all its peers have moved higher up the avenue; but if it's a bit *too* old-school there's Lord and Taylor not far away, which is more fun perhaps, or we can go to Saks, which is swishier, or Bonwit Teller, which is trendier, or up to Bloomingdale's beneath the El, if we really must, or down to Lane Bryant if despite the rationing at home we are of unusually generous figure. All too quickly the afternoon passes, leaving us only half an hour at the Museum of Modern Art before we return to the Plaza (tip of the hat and complicit smile from the doorman) to dump our delectably ribboned parcels on the beds, take off our shoes and order a couple of martinis.

How to spend the evening? There is no limit. We

can go to the Philharmonic at Carnegie Hall, we *might* one supposes get a ticket for *La Traviata* at the Met, we'd love to catch that *Harvey*, we wouldn't mind seeing the Lunts again though we saw them in fact in that very same play in London during the blitz . . . But no, we will be true to the times and the city, do what Gloria and her friend would do, and go to one of the great Broadway movie houses to see a Star on Stage. Paramount, Roxy, Capitol, Strand—they are all terrific, all prodigies of plush and bright lights, all household names, but the most terrific, most brightly-lit, plushiest and best-known of all is Radio City Music Hall in Rockefeller Center, the biggest theatre in the world. Even we know all about Radio City Music Hall. Its air-conditioning is laced with ozone, to make us feel happier.[1] Its organ is the largest ever built. Its auditorium is egg-shaped. Its men's smoking room is decorated in aluminum foil. Its stage-elevators are so powerful that the U.S. Navy has adapted them for aircraft carriers. Its Rockette chorus girls live like odalisques in dormitories backstage.[2] John D. Rockefeller, Jr., himself, sur-

---

[1] But not with laughing-gas as its creator, the supreme impresario Samuel Rothafel ("Roxy") had originally proposed.

[2] Sometimes to spend the best part of a lifetime there—one member of the troupe in 1945 did not retire until she was sixty, and chorines in their fifties were not uncommon. Nowadays they live at home, and the dormitories are dressing rooms, but otherwise the theatre, renamed the Music Hall Entertainment Center, is much as it was.

veying this improbable product of his wealth, has declared it "beautiful, soul-satisfying, inspiring beyond anything I have dreamed possible." To the Music Hall it is then, "Where the Fun Never Sets," and after the Rockettes and the movie to the climax of our evening on the town, the arrival on that stupendous stage of the show's stupendous star, whose name is displayed so gigantically in lights outside, and whose aura is all but mystical.

And since we are looking for archetypes, or essences, we must put up there if only in our fancy, from all the galaxy of celebrated performers on the stages of Manhattan tonight, the starriest star of them all, Sinatra. He is a New Yorker true and tried, though a New Jersey boy, and his figure, elegant but somehow louche, his trembling lower lip and tilted hat, the slow behind-the-beat languor of his love songs, all exactly satisfies Manhattan's own view of itself, and confirms our own. As he swings into "All or Nothing at All," to a mingled gasp, sigh and muffled scream from around the vast auditorium, we somehow feel we have ourselves made it to the Big Time.

Borscht at the Russian Bear perhaps, or frogs' legs and meringues at Le Pavillon, an hour with the jazz at Open Door, a nightcap at the Monkey Bar, and up the glittering avenue we stroll once more to the great hotel beside the park, where the old barouches are still labouring up and down, drivers bent skew-whiff on their seats to talk to the tourists behind, and the former coachman to the Cornelius Vanderbilt IIs, recognizing us in the streetlight, doffs his tall hat in our direction. Shall we ever forget our day of pleasure in Manhattan as, with the city still pulsing and singing and laughing outside our windows, and the howl of the police cars penetrating even the calm of the Plaza's fifteenth floor, we prepare ourselves excitedly (for we are not in the least tired) for bed?

What a day! Fortune smiled and came my way!
I could laugh out loud,
I'm so lucky to be me . . .

7

On Purposes

BUT THOSE HOWLING SIRENS, which reach us intermittently through the night, until they merge with the grind and clatter of the garbage trucks in the small hours—those harsh noises off are a reminder that Manhattan is not just a city of delight. The pleasure is peripheral to the deeper objects of the place, which are thrusting, inexorable, noble and sometimes nasty. This is the most hopeful city on earth, but the most demanding; the most tolerant but the most competitive. It is also the most intensely concentrated, and within its confines there is hardly a trade, hardly a profession, hardly a commodity, hardly a mode of business that cannot be found. Other cities can claim the same, but none since Venice have jammed all their purposes between such tight and explicit boundaries.

Traditional

Manhattan had been a place of consequence for nearly three hundred years, and it had acted as a catalyst for traditions far older. For all its vigor it did not feel a young city, like the cities of the American West, and not all its activities were, so to speak, streamlined. Some were as gnarled as anything to be found in the ancient burghs of Europe or Asia. The oldest business in town was claimed to be a paint manufacturers, Devoe and Raynolds of 787 First Avenue, which had started in 1754, at the foot of Water Street, and whose trademark showed a feathered Indian with a pestle labelled "The First American Paint Maker."[1] Here are a few other firms, occupations and institutions still bucking the trends in Manhattan, 1945:

o The Fifth Avenue Bank, occupying three old brownstone houses on the corner of 44th Street, specialized in the accounts of elderly dowagers. It had a

_____

[1] Since the 1970s its local premises have been over the water in Hoboken, New Jersey, and in the way of corporate development, its head office is now in Louisville, Kentucky.

brocaded banking room reserved for lady clients (allegedly so that they could without embarrassment remove folding money from their stocking tops), and employed a ladies' maid to serve them tea. At Christmas that year the bank received a card from an elderly client, Miss Pratt, which said: "Dear Bank, I just got your calendar, and I just got to thinking, I'll bet nobody ever sends you a Christmas card, personal like. Thanks for being a nice, gracious bank with good taste."

o On East 79th Street the New York Society Library, founded in 1754 to be "useful as well as ornamental to the city," lived in a splendid Italianate town house and offered its members 175,000 books and every reading comfort; on East 47th Street the Mercantile Library, founded in 1820 and known familiarly as The Merc, offered its members 200,000 books, a Writers' Studio in which Edgar Allan Poe had worked and a monthly lecture series begun by Ralph Waldo Emerson.

o The Stoeger Arms Corporation, on Fifth Avenue in midtown, was one of the few gunsmiths left in the world specializing in flintlock guns, which it sold in large quantities to Africans denied more modern weapons by colonial governments.

o George M. Still, Inc., dealers in Diamond Point oysters, operated the oyster barge *George M. Still*, which lay at the foot of Pike Street below Manhattan Bridge. The one survivor of a succession of flamboyant craft from which, over many generations, the citizens of Manhattan had bought their oysters, it was loudly painted in yellow, orange, green, black and white, had a grand balcony on its upper deck, and flew from its mast a long swallow-tailed pennant labelled G. M. Still, Inc.

o Simpson's the pawnbroking firm of Park Row, founded in 1882, had made a great deal of money from the proximity of Chinatown, whose gamblers always needed cash, and had advanced funds to many celebrities—when in 1932 the Hope Diamond was put in hock to raise the ransom for the kidnapped Lindbergh baby, it was Simpson's who advanced $36,750 on it (making it was said only twenty cents profit on the deal). Its directors were related, by blood or by marriage, to most of the other leading Manhattan pawnbrokers, among them Rothman's on Eighth Avenue, famous for its gigantic cluster of golden balls and its slogan "BROKE—CALL ON UNCLE."

o It was the vocation of Mr. James Patrick Kelly ("Smelly" Kelly, or "Leaky" Kelly) to patrol the IND subway tracks sniffing out gas leaks. He had been doing it for twenty-five years, and was celebrated for having once identified the cause of a most peculiar smell at the 42nd Street station—elephant dung from the garbage cans of the Hippodrome at 43rd and Sixth Avenue, where they used to have circuses.

o Klein's on Union Square had been founded in the previous century as the original self-service store, without salesgirls at counters, only supervisors on high stools. It had hardly changed in 1945; you still chose your clothes from the innumerable racks in a cavernous shopping area, and tried them on in a communal changing-room beneath huge signs warning you in English, Italian and Yiddish: "DO NOT DISGRACE YOUR FAMILY. THE PUNISHMENT FOR STEALING IS JAIL."

o The New York Diamond Market, one of the most important in the world, was run by Jews, many of them rigidly Orthodox, in a clutter of contiguous buildings around the corner of Canal Street and the Bowery. Auctions were silent and secretive affairs, bids often being made by a touch on the auctioneer's knee or shoulder, and much business was done in the street outside. There a dealer might have in his vest pocket his entire stock in trade—one diamond very possibly, which he would stealthily withdraw, wrapped in a handkerchief, when a deal was in the offing. All down the sidewalk one might see such furtive movements, negotiations conducted vest-to-vest almost, surreptitious flickings of fingers or jerking of heads, as the almost incalculable wealth of the market passed from hand to hand, account to account, and sometimes continent to continent.

o Olliffe's Apothecary had been selling its proprietory formulae on the Bowery since the days when that was a fashionable part of town: its pharmacists were still mixing and marketing the identical specifics that had made the original Dr. Olliffe famous in the first years of the nineteenth century.

o Steinway's, who built their pianos out on Long Island, since 1925 had sold and rented them from their showrooms, Steinway Hall, on West 57th Street. Upstairs there was a circular salon, with a chandelier, marble pillars and painted scenes of musical import;

downstairs was the "piano bank," where the great pianists of the world came to choose the instruments for their performances, and where Horowitz and Rachmaninoff were once seen playing poker together among the assembled concert grands.

There were many, many more. Meyer Berger of the *New York Times*, who loved all nooky trades and callings, interviewed scores of curious merchants and artificers for his weekly column: ostrich-egg agents and importers of armadillo meat, dealers in medical leeches, medieval-style engravers, monkish bookbinders and the man who serviced most of Manhattan's church clocks (when clocks had to be changed each year for daylight saving time, he worked for two nights and days solid to get them done). There was a shop on Third Avenue that made working models for amateur inventors. Tea-leaf readers were readily available. On 42nd Street a man with a telescope offered views of the planet Saturn and the Empire State Building, with particular focus on the eightieth floor, where the bomber had crashed. Such activities were hardly what one expected of Manhattan, the Wonder City, but they were a reminder that this was a city linked by tough strains of custom and heredity with older societies far away.[1]

---

[1] The two grand old libraries flourish still. Simpson's are now in Trinity Place, conveniently next door to the American Stock Exchange. Steinway Hall is just the same, and is still frequented by virtuosi. Klein's lingered on for another three decades, but

Salesmanship

Selling things was Manhattan's most obvious business, and excessive salesmanship was part of the city ethos. "More than three billion dollars are spent each year," said the editors of the *Look* guidebook, "in New York's retail stores, for live turtles, evening gowns, airplanes and other paraphernalia." Manhattan sold everything, and in a manner all its own.

The world's chief seller of beauty, for example, was undoubtedly the Du Barry Success School, 693 Fifth Avenue. Its celebrated Before and After pictures, demonstrating the results of a course at the school, had a magnetic effect upon passers-by, and had become legendary throughout the country—the school claimed that among every hundred American women between the ages of sixteen and sixty, one had taken the Du Barry Home Success Course, and twelve had asked for details.

---

when I asked after it in 1985, a man pointed to a corner of Union Square and said: "Ya see that hole in the ground? That's Klein's." The diamond quarter has shifted to West 47th Street, between Fifth and Sixth Avenues, where its dealers now include some Jews from Bombay, but a few traditionalists have stayed on the Bowery. Tea-leaf readers remain popular, and though the telescope man has left 42nd Street the sidewalks of Manhattan proliferate now with a kaleidoscopic variety of traders, pedlars and performers.

The most magical purveyor of gadgetry was Hammacher Schlemmer's on East 57th Street, which had been selling high-class gimmickry since 1848, and whose range of arcane trinkets and devices would perfectly have satisfied Emperors of China or Czars in St. Petersburg. The champion sellers of neon signs were beyond all doubt Artkraft Strauss. They had started in 1897, with gas-illuminated advertisements, and in their workshops below the West Side Highway they had made all the most stunning of the Times Square signs; their celebrated designer Douglas Leigh had recently suggested turning the entire summit of the Empire State Building into a gigantic Coke bottle.[1] And where else could be the sales headquarters of Wurlitzers, makers of all those Mighty Organs in Ritzes, Odeons, Carltons, Majestics, Regals and Rialtos across the world—where else but 130 West 42nd Street, New York, New York?

The great department stores were unmistakably Manhattan in style. McCreery's defined itself as being "King-Sized But Personal," and engraved in gold on a pillar in the ground floor of Wanamaker's was an apothegm by its founder John Wanamaker: "LET THOSE WHO FOLLOW ME CONTINUE TO BUILD WITH THE PLUMB OF HONOR, THE LEVEL OF TRUTH AND THE SQUARE OF INTEGRITY,

---

[1] In 1977, instead, he designed the pioneering floodlight system which now illuminates the building from the seventy-second floor to the summit, and which has since been emulated on many other skyscrapers.

EDUCATION, COURTESY AND MUTUALITY."[1]
This was of course just window-dressing. The Manhattan stores did not wish to be your best friends, they
wished to take your money, and they were not invariably
attached to the square of integrity. The vernacular
phrase "I'd rather work in Macy's basement" meant that
you'd almost rather die, and Robert Moses once blamed
most of the city's financial problems upon the stubborn
selfishness and deception of its business community.
Still, the flair, push and ingenuity of the shops did im-
measurably contribute to Manhattan's sparkle.

This was the town of the very latest store dummies
(modelled, in 1945, less and less on the Duchess of
Windsor and Greta Garbo, more and more on Greer
Garson and Joan Crawford). This is where comparison
shopping was invented. Macy's Thanksgiving Day Parade, which started as a pure publicity display, had become one of the great civic events of the year; often
a million people watched its progress from Central Park
West to Herald Square, four hundred clowns pranced
all the way, and its gigantic blow-up elephants and
Mickey Mouses floated above the streets like heroic
trophies in a triumph. This was the town of store slogans, as familiar as TV advertising jingles would later

---

[1] Masonic sentiments which did not, alas, prevent the store's dis-
appearance from Manhattan (though the Eternal Light, a World
War I memorial presented by the Wanamakers to the city of
New York, still burns in the star at the top of its column in
Madison Square).

be: "Nobody, But Nobody, Undersells Us" (Gimbel's), "It Pays To Be Thrifty" (Macy's), "A Business in Millions . . . A Profit in Pennies" (Ohrbach's).[1]

Their sales and advertising techniques were wonderfully persuasive. No matter where you bought your shirt, Wallachs would give you a free button—sew it on, too—if one came off. McCreery's advertised on its roof for the benefit of people in skyscrapers. Macy's sent parcels about by roller-skate messengers, and ran a Ski Information Bureau which not only booked hotels and tickets for you, but woke you up in the morning in time to catch the early ski trains. Gimbel's breezily exploited its old rivalry with Macy's, a step or two away across Herald Square—"Does Macy's Tell Gimbel's?" their advertisements used to sneer, when Macy's came out with some new claim to supremacy, "Does Gimbel's Tell Macy's? *No, Gimbel's Tells the World!*" At Christmas time the competition between the stores was famously intense, and innumerable Santa Clauses rivalled each other's ho-ho-hos: a familiar story told of a small boy, having informed one incumbent what presents he wanted for Christmas, being confronted by another. "And what would you like for Christmas?" asks the old gentleman. "You silly old man," the boy replies. "I knew you'd forget."

The wealth and luxury of the great stores was pro-

---

[1] Both "Nobody, But Nobody . . . " and "It Pays To Be Thrifty" were coined by the copywriter Bernice Fitzgibbon, a former English teacher who had worked first for Macy's, then for Gimbels.

digious, and to the stranger from Europe in those post-war months a visit to any one of these grand emporia,[1] so scented and warm, so ribboned and colorful, so heaped with inconceivable profusions of goods, was like an experience more fabulous than real, expressing morals either of consolation or of despair, depending upon how soon you had to return to the austerities of home.

The Quarters

Manhattan had often suggested to writers an oriental city. O. Henry had called it "Baghdad upon the Subways," and in a protracted fancy Felix Reisenberg once likened a trip down Broadway to a pilgrimage to Mecca ("At high meridian our thirsting incontinent camels have slunk into a side bodega . . ."). Suggestively Eastern certainly was the city's predeliction for merchants' quarters. As in the souks of Cairo or Damascus, and in much the same spirit, craftsmen, merchants and entrepreneurs tended to bunch together by trade or commodity.

---

[1] Or Grand Emporiums, as is robustly preferred by Robert Hendrickson in his entertaining book of that name (1978), to which I am indebted for much of this commercial intelligence. Even as I write, by the way, one of the grandest of them, Gimbel's, is closing its doors for ever.

Thus purveyors of bridal gowns were clustered on Grand Street, on the Lower East Side, where they were open seven days a week, and leather workers congregated under the arches of Manhattan Bridge. Fourth Avenue around Union Square was the place for book-sellers, one after the other down the sidewalks: Weiser's, the Pageant, Tannen's, some neat and scholarly, some as untidy, dusty, fragrant with old paper and decaying leather as the most dedicated browser could demand. In the Fur District, with its epicenter roughly at Seventh Avenue and West 28th Street, fifteen thousand workers were hard at it on the minks and sables of prosperity. The neighbouring Garment District was enjoying boom times too, and was one of the most distinctive quarters of all. It had evolved from the evil old sweatshops of the Lower East Side, and was still a warren of small factories and wholesale shops, through whose ever-crowded streets racks of ready-mades were deftly maneuvered by "push-boys" black and white, while steam from the pressing-machines billowed out of upstairs windows, and massive ugly delivery trucks, hooting and reverberating, blocked the thoroughfares and were frequently humped lop-sided over sidewalks.

Barbers' schools abounded along the Bowery, offering dirt-cheap back-and-side cuts if a customer cared to take a risk. So did tattooists and specialists in disguising black eyes. Music publishers and songwriters liked to find offices in the Brill Building, a smoke-blackened old structure on Broadway which they shared with boxing managements. For everything to do with fruit and vegetables, you must go to the area loosely called the Washington Market, on the Lower West Side, into whose purlieus the city's fresh victuals poured every night by truck, by train, in scows across the Hudson River and in the pick-ups of Long Island market gardeners (it used to be said that if all Manhattan's food had to come in by rail, it would need a train twenty-five miles long every day of the year). For everything to do with fish, you must go across town to the most celebrated of all Manhattan's marts, the Fulton Street Fish Market on the East River, almost in the shadow of Brooklyn Bridge.

This, if you got there sufficiently early in the morning, was one of the great mercantile spectacles of New York. The market was furiously busy then. A myriad Kings of the Sea and Ship-A-Hoys meant that its turnover was probably greater than that of any other fish market on earth, and it was also full of hoary character, having operated on more or less the same site since the days of the Dutch. In 1945, though much of its produce came in refrigerated trucks from New England or the New Jersey shore towns, some was still brought directly to the market quays by fishing boats; and the sight of their masts and sails—the last commercial sails to be seen in New York harbor—movingly expressed the exactness, the compactness and the continuity of Manhattan.

Many of the fishmongers were Italian, and the market was rather Mediterranean in feel, though with a very un-Latin range of merchandise; not the bright transparencies and phosphorescences of the warm seas, but mostly stolid northern creatures like cod and Maine lobsters, oysters from New England, clams, shad, sea bass, stone crabs, flatfish from the Atlantic seabeds, herring, Canadian salmon, hefty red slabs of tunny to be chopped about by fishwives. All around the market were fishy places too: fish retailers, fish brokers, bars where the fish men drank, restaurants like Sweets and Sloppy Louie's and shadowy cobbled fish-smelling corners where the truck-drivers, having delivered their crustaceans from the north or Florida red snapper, snatched a few hours' sleep in their cabs before the long drive home.[1]

Images

Indefatigably around the Times Square Tower revolved the Motogram, spelling out the day's news in its thousands of bulbs (it worked by the passing of five-

---

[1] Gone, the Bowery barber-schools, the Manhattan Bridge leatherworkers, the Washington Market, whose site is now called TriBeCa (the Triangle Below Canal) and is very trendy, and most of the Fourth Avenue booksellers. Reduced, the Garment District, now undergoing hard times, the Fur District, its work force reduced to less than three thousand, and the Grand Street bridal shops, subsumed by Chinatown and sometimes turned into *Chinese* bridal shops. In fine form, the Fulton Street Fish Market, successfully defying the South Street Seaport Museum development, Sweets and Sloppy Louie's, now both gone up-market.

foot-high individual letters over electrified wire brushes),
It had been built in 1928, and ever since then, except
during the dim-out, Mr. Edward Linder and Mr. James
Torpey had been operating the electric text up there,
every night of the year between twilight and midnight:
so adept were they at inserting the letters on their chain
conveyor that they could get a news story up in lights
within three minutes of its arrival at the *Times* editorial offices across the way.[1] If you wanted to choose a
single symbol for the purposes of Manhattan, the Motogram might provide it: inexorable, always on the move,
dedicated, endlessly communicative. It sometimes
seemed that the chief point of this city was self-
advertisement. A blind man would know he was in New
York from the endless chatter of it; a deaf man could
hardly escape the Motogram and its myriad siblings of
the information (and mis-information) industry.

Words, messages, themes, quotations, slogans, logos,
rumors, assertions, refutations, confirmations, enquiries,
dispatches, enumerations, slanders, lies, hard facts and
images—above all perhaps images true and false: all
these were the stuff of Manhattan. Ten major daily newspapers in English were published on the island,[2] and

---

[1] They had helped to build the device, and they worked it together for thirty-three years until the *Times* sold the building in
1961. Five years later they died within a few months of each other,
Mr. Torpey aged seventy, Mr. Linder (in a car crash) seventy-two.

[2] *Herald-Tribune, Journal-American, Journal of Commerce, News,
Post, P.M., Sun, Times, Wall Street Journal, World-Telegram.*

several more in foreign languages, together with hundreds of weeklies, monthlies and quarterlies eminent and obscure. There were 350 publishers of one sort or another, seventy literary agents each as rich as the next, and forty book clubs. The city crawled with writers, Heaven knows, but it was richer still in editors, and richest of all in advertising managers.

In those days old-school publishers still had their offices downtown,[1] in the traditional publishing quarter around Union Square—the stretch of Fourth Avenue between the Square and 34th Street was nicknamed Publishers' Row. Here, as in London, publishing in those days was a very gentlemanly occupation. Lofty houses like Knopf and Harper's were associated with the greatest names of American literature, and their publishers moved lordly through the literary world, appearing like *dei ex machina* at launching parties, and subserviently courted by visiting colleagues from Europe. They produced beautiful books on thick expensive paper, printed in grand old typefaces with ink of a particularly American, or to imaginative bibliophiles even a particularly Manhattan smell.[2]

---

[1] Some of them are going back there now, driven away from midtown by impossible rents.

[2] Bibliophiles like me: there are books I bought more than thirty years ago which can still, by a single sniff of their pages, transport me instantly over the ocean to New York. Books don't smell like that any more.

Most of the great daily newspapers, however, had abandoned their old downtown offices, and moved to flashier quarters further north. There had once been twelve daily newspapers in the streets around Park Row, four of them side by side. The *Sun* was still down there, but the *Times* was now off Times Square, the *Herald-Tribune* was in Herald Square, the *Daily News* had built itself a famous skyscraper in midtown, and all the others, radical *P.M.* to true-blue *Wall Street Journal*, were scattered here and there across the island. There was no Manhattan Fleet Street now.[1]

Fitfully there flourished, nevertheless, the club-like world of journalism which had been so characteristic of Manhattan in the 1920s and 1930s, when the press had clustered around City Hall and Tammany, and newspaper writers like Ring Lardner and Damon Runyon had created a genre not merely of art, but almost of life. Reporters were still Hemingways in hope, sub-editors undiscovered O. Henrys—an early career on the press remained a recognized avenue into the literary life. Newspapermen gathered fraternally at Bleeck's or McSorley's, and you might still observe, if dimly, the world of the copyroom made famous by film and novel, the

---

[1] Of the old newspaper quarter, which had been the largest aggregate of press offices in the world, the only relics today are the *Sun* clock still on the corner of Chambers and Broadway ("The Sun—It Shines for All"), and the original Park Row office of the *Times*, now part of Pace University.

world of cynical city editor and ambitious copyboy, the eyeshade, the mackintosh, the hat with the press ticket in it, the big Speed Graphic camera and the upright Remington. A hero of the day was Ernie Pyle, a Scripps-Howard war correspondent who had been killed that spring in the Okinawa fighting—everybody's idea of a New York newspaperman, tough but unpretentious, sentimental but no respecter of persons, and expressing himself in a forceful no-nonsense style that every cab-driver appreciated.

Except for the war correspondents, though, by 1945 the stars of newspaper journalism were no longer the reporters of legend, but columnists—pundits of one sort or another, like Walter Lippmann, Westbrook Pegler or Drew Pearson, gossips like Winchell and Lyons, Ed Sullivan whose column was called "Little Ol' New York," Elsa Maxwell, Cholly Knickerbocker of the *Journal-American* whose real name was Igor Cassini, and who had once been tarred and feathered in Virginia for his disparaging remarks about Southern womanhood. The gossip writers, in particular, depended upon a breathless technique of quip and punctuation. Here is Ed Sullivan one evening that summer: "Hotel Astor operators going nuts with Joan Barry and Gracie Barrie registered . . . Lou Walters bedded with a touch of grippe . . . Frank Dailey and Jimmy Dorsey kissed and made up." And here is a characteristic item from Dan Walker: "If Peggy Hopkins Joyce is 39, then she was born in 1906, which means that her first marriage, annulled in 1912, happened when she was six."

They were oddly gauche techniques, and in many ways the Manhattan newspaper press feels, in retrospect, miles behind the city times. The doyen of its papers was the *Times*, and it had not greatly changed, in manner at least, since its acquisition in the previous century by the Ochs family from Tennessee. Very conservative New Yorkers hardly thought of it as a local institution even then, and liked to say that it was "run by people from the South." Its slogan "All the News That's Fit to Print" had been on its masthead since 1896, and its offices on West 43rd Street included a library in Elizabethan style, with leaded windows.[1] The breezy tabloids could be astonishingly archaic, not least in their fondness for positively Victorian serial stories. Here is a typical extract from *With Bated Breath*, by Alice Campbell, which was running in the *News* that summer: "It really did seem an insoluble riddle, Lady Barkdale raced on, not the least weird feature being the fatal disappearance of the Woman on the Bus. What woman? Why, the strange woman who had shared Aggie's front seat!" Even the bizarre vocabulary of *Variety*, the peri-

---

[1] Forty years on the almost unchanging format and formulae of the *Times* give the microfilm reader a melancholy sense of *après-vu*—those young brides of 1945, now so mature and all too probably so divorced, those promising Books of the Times, reviewed so exactly as they review the literary hopefuls of today, alas so often long forgotten . . . The masthead slogan was devised by Adolph Ochs himself, and triumphs still over thousands of suggested alternatives, among them "Free from Filth, Full of News."

odical of show business, harked back to an earlier world
of vernacular journalism, laced as it was with Jewish
pith and wisecrack. "Disk Jockey," "Showbiz" and
"Niteries" were all *Variety* innovations, reviews were
Offish or Terrif, Crix might Nix Drama, or give it
Sockeroo, delays in Skeds might cause Squawk from Star
or even lead to PHFFT Decish . . .[1]

Ageing too, if rather before its time, was the fascina-
tion of the *New Yorker* magazine. This famous organ
of urbanity was actually only twenty years old, having
been founded shortly before the Wall Street crash in
the same 43rd Street office where it still functioned, but
it seemed to many of its readers more or less traditional
to New York. "No city in the world," it said of itself in
one of its advertisements, "not London, not Paris, not
Rome, not Vienna, has, or ever has had, a magazine of
its own like *The New Yorker*, bearing its name and
focussed sharply on its doings." Suave, mannered, a
little precious, extremely clever, often wonderfully
funny, the *New Yorker* felt very much of the 1930s, even
of the 1920s, and had spawned a literary circle of its
own, in the prewar style, which met under the aegis of
its formidable editor, Harold Ross, at the Algonquin
Hotel on East 44th Street. The Round Table had been
splintered by war and age, but some of its original mem-

---

[1] In other words reviews were half-hearted or enthusiastic, critics
might deplore or acclaim a play, while delays in production
schedules might anger a leading performer or result in a decision
to abandon the project.

bers were still around, and the Algonquin profited greatly from the legend of Dorothy Parker's wit or the chance of Robert Benchley's presence.[1]

But there was nothing nostalgic about *Life* magazine, the most brilliant journalistic phenomenon of Manhattan in 1945. *Life* was at the very peak of its success—the criterion of photojournalism, copied all over the world. Forty years later it would be hard to conceive how influential such a picture magazine could be, and how absolutely it commanded the talents of a generation. Every photographer wanted to be in *Life*, every model coveted its cover, few writers, however eminent, would decline an invitation to contribute an essay to it, and its features were as common a subject of party conversation as a hit television series in later decades. It influenced events, but it also faithfully reflected them, and its style, the look of it, the shape of it, its choice of words, was a crystalization of contemporary Manhattan taste. *Life*'s offices were at 1 Rockefeller Plaza, the most modern place to be, but so conscious was it of its image that it declined all exterior decoration, declined even one of the more striking buildings of the Center complex, in case the force of its own personality might be compromised. Everything about *Life* had to be unique, and it managed to mould the skills of its contributors,

---

[1] As it does to this day, though Stephen Brook says of it in his irresistible *New York Days, New York Nights* (1985): "The Algonquin is supposed to be packed with celebrities, but apart from myself I've never spotted a soul."

and especially its corps of photographers, into a true stylistic unity.

In 1945 an average issue of *Life* contained rather more than one hundred shiny pages—big pages, for its shape was almost that of a tabloid newspaper—with pictures on most pages, some of them in color. The magazine had set the fashion for the protracted masthead later to be thought essential by any self-respecting American magazine: *Life* listed, below its Editor-in-Chief and Proprietor, Henry R. Luce, no fewer than 151 editorial staff members, including the twenty-one researchers who were supposed to make its accuracy infallible. It might have twenty or so pages of news reportage, mostly pictorial—strikes in the Middle West, early meetings of the United Nations organization in San Francisco, a parade of returning soldiers down Fifth Avenue. It would probably have a long portrait of some celebrity in the news, and an essay about a foreign country perhaps, or an industry, sometimes illustrated lavishly with specially commissioned paintings. There might be one of the famous *Life Goes to a Party* features, reporting anything from a high school graduation dance to an Army Fliers' Take-off Party—the magazine often covered half a dozen festivities, at home and abroad, before its editors decided which one to use. A theatre review, a bit of Hollywood gossip, some letters, a little outré feature like the story of Mr. Elliott E. Simpson and his parrot, and that was that. It does not sound very startling, and its editorial comment, dictated no doubt by Mr. Luce, was unlikely to be illuminating: but it was done with immense panache, and it properly reflected the Manhattan life that throbbed about its midtown offices—shiny, efficient, punchy and assured.[1]

On the Air

Yet no amount of punch or assurance, no number of beers at Bleeck's or martinis in the Oak Room of the Algonquin, could protect the newspaper and magazine industry from the advance of electronics, of which Manhattan was beyond all dispute the world headquarters— the hometown of radio, as somebody called it then (Rockefeller Center itself was originally to have been named Radio City, hence Radio City Music Hall). Everything that was newest, brightest and richest in radio was centred upon this island. Television, vestigially started before the war, was in abeyance, confined to closed circuits and experimentation as the networks feverishly raced each other to launch a full public service, but radio was ubiquitous. Its performers were superstars. Its catch-phrases were on every lip. Its four great networks—Mutual, NBC, ABC, CBS—were powers of the city.

---

[1] The weekly *Life* closed in 1972: the bi-weekly version which came later was a very different thing.

Manhattan radio in 1945 suggests in retrospect a weird blend of the advanced and the adolescent. There were eminent commentators—Edward R. Murrow, Raymond Gram Swing, William L. Schirer, Max Lerner—who provided serious interpretations of world events. There were frequent news broadcasts, some of them almost stately in style, and many classical concerts: every Saturday afternoon there was a matinee broadcast from the Met,[1] with an Opera Quiz in the intermission, and a panel discussion. On the other hand, there was a plethora of almost infantile entertainment at almost all hours of day or night, interrupted by advertisements of puerile invention—"FLY-DED, the Modern Spray in Every Way," or "BISODOL, Best for Gastric-Hyper-Acidity, Often Called American Stomach," delivered more often than not in a vibrant male voice, without music.

All day long you could listen to soap operas (as they were already called, originally by broadcasters themselves because they were generally sponsored by soap companies). "Young Dr. Malone," "The Road of Life," "Just Plain Bill, the real life story of someone who might be your neighbour"—at any moment, as you did the housework or took time off for coffee you might hear the lugubrious electric organ music that introduced them, and the preternaturally careful diction of their actors. Half of them were written by the unchallenged queen of the genre, Irna Phillips, whose dictum was

---

[1] As there still is—same sponsor (1986), same producer.

"Life is a daytime serial, escape it if you can." Her work was replete in nervous breakdowns, husband-murders, illegitimacies revealed, child adoptions, custody disputes and esoteric medical problems, and was to have a decisive influence on mass entertainment apparently for ever afterwards.

Two programs outranked even the Irna Phillips soaps, however, in popularity. At 11 a.m., each morning, Eastern Standard Time being what it was, New Yorkers by the million tuned in to ABC's "Breakfast in Hollywood," an hour of gush and banter with a former vaudeville singer called Tom Breneman. And on Saturdays there was the smash quiz show "Truth or Consequences," with its thrillingly accumulating jackpot. At the end of 1945 this prize was to be won by correctly identifying a mystery voice (Jack Dempsey's, actually) reciting "Hickory-Dickory-Dock"; it comprised by then a refrigerator, a vacuum cleaner, a washing machine, a gas range, a radio-phonograph with one hundred records, a piano, a complete man's wardrobe, twenty-four pairs of nylon stockings, a diamond ring, a diamond and ruby wristwatch, a silver fox fur coat, a weekend at the Waldorf, a round air trip from New York to Los Angeles, two weeks in the Canadian Rockies, a new-model Mercury car and a maid's services for a year.[1]

The radio provided, as the publicists used to say, one long Miracle of Easy Listening. There was never a dull

---

[1] All fell into the lap of Ensign Richard Bartholomew, USN, of Arkansas.

moment. After Lowell Thomas on the Far Places of the Earth, after Hymns of All Churches and Tom Mix and Bob Hope, very soon it was time for "Front Page Farrell, the Story of a Crack Newspaperman," or Drew Pearson presenting "This Is Your FBI"—and that took you through to the Rudy Vallee Show, and Abbott and Costello, and André Kostelanetz in "Music Millions Love," and the March of Time, and Charlie Chan, and Dick Tracy himself . . . "Listen, your Mother and I remember when there was nothin' more than a couple of bum programs a day, and more crackle than sense then, and we had to take those goddam accumulators round to Scheltman the electrician, used to be down there on the corner 21st and Seventh, to get 'em charged up. Now that's *progress!*"

(But just around the corner television was awaiting its turn. The Waldorf-Astoria was all wired up for it, and in many a plush apartment you might see the tiny round-cornered screen, mounted in monstrous column of walnut or mahogany, only waiting for its picture.)

Art

Manhattan had long prided itself on its artistic purposes. Its museums and galleries were legendary, its patrons and patronesses matchlessly lavish. It had been a city of music always—one of the great European war aims, the violinist Yehudi Menuhin once said, was to get to New York. It was a hive of writers, and among those working in Manhattan then (to choose a few names at random) were Arthur Miller, Damon Runyon, John Cheever, John Steinbeck, Bertolt Brecht, e. e. cummings, W. H. Auden, James Baldwin and Tennessee Williams —could any other 14,000 acres boast of such a roster?[1]

In the visual arts Manhattan was now about to achieve a startling new prominence. In the Museum of Modern Art there hung in those days Picasso's epic picture *Guernica*, perhaps the truest of all representations of the age. The removal of this picture to New York in 1939 was Picasso's political gesture against Franco's government in Spain, but it was seen too as symbolical of art's own movement: westward, away from worked-out Europe, into the fresh and futurist New World. A host of great European artists had come with it, Surrealists and Abstractionists from Chagall to Salvador Dali, and

---

[1] Miller's *The Man Who Had All the Luck* had opened in 1944 and lasted four performances. Williams's *The Glass Menagerie* opened in 1945 and made his fortune. Steinbeck thought that if you had once lived in Manhattan "no place else is good enough." Brecht's telephone was tapped by the FBI. Runyon's ashes were scattered from an aircraft over Times Square when he died in 1946. A plaque in St. Mark's Place, where Auden was to live for twenty years, quotes his apothegm: *If equal affection cannot be/ Let the more loving one be me.* John Cheever would one day be the laureate of Manhattan in these postwar years—"a long-lost world when the city of New York was still filled with river light . . . and when almost everybody wore a hat."

had already made New York the adopted center of their several movements.

Before the war the artists of Manhattan had seen themselves as decidedly second-string to the Parisians. So had the Parisians. When a huge collection of American art was shown in France in the 1930s it had been given a contemptuous reception by the critics—its only merit, one said, was "an originality that accentuates the indecency of its arrogance. . . ." Most of the Manhattan art galleries had then been run by Frenchmen, scornful of the local product, and when the organizers of the World's Fair had asked "What will tomorrow's world be like?" the text that accompanied the French art exhibition had replied frankly enough: "Like yesterday's and today's, very largely of French inspiration." Even the editors of the *Partisan Review*, in those prewar years the chief mouthpiece of the Manhattan intelligentsia, had decided that only a Europeanization of culture could vitalize American art.

By 1945 it had dawned upon Manhattan that in art as in all else Europe was no longer the be-all and end-all, and there was developing in the city an indigenous school of art, the first to be evolved upon American soil. Some of its originators were transplanted Europeans who had enthusiastically adopted the feel of America, as artists so often did. George Grosz the German Dadaist had declared himself an admirer of Norman Rockwell. Piet Mondrian from Holland had called his last, unfinished picture *Victory Boogie-Woogie*. Hans Hofmann from Germany had established an influential art school on East 8th Street, and the Dutch-born Willem de Kooning was a leading member of the American avant-garde. Fired by the sympathetic presence of such masters, there came into being the New York School, which was presently to offer a new focus for artists everywhere, just as the Parisians had before the war. It was hardly a school really in the old artistic sense. Its members were often friends as well as colleagues, frequenting particular taverns, finding themselves studios mostly around East 10th Street near Washington Square, but they had no recognizable common style or program. Their only hallmark was their extreme energy and aggressiveness—their conception of a picture not just as an image but as an act. They drew impartially upon the several European schools as few Europeans would, and they turned also to ritualism, to myth, and to the pre-Columbian heritage. Their pictures were frequently disjointed and disturbing, reminding some people of the furious disintegration of atoms, and others of the headlong, helter-skelter momentum of Manhattan itself.

The archetype among them was the Wyoming-born Jackson Pollock, a melancholy and neurotic alcoholic who had lived in the city many years, who was haunted by Picasso's *Guernica*, and who was as violent when drunk as he was gentle when sober. Pollock was the master of Action Painting, a method of throwing paint onto an unstretched canvas laid out on the floor, thereby producing the huge swirling patterns of primary colors, maze-like and violent, which the world would always associate with postwar Manhattan. He derived some of his inspiration from the Indian sand-painters of the West, who allowed sand of various colors to trickle into mystic shapes, and his pictures too had an element to them of fateful intervention. They represented nothing at all but his own emotions as he made them, or the unseen forces that were impelling him, and he painted them sometimes in a kind of frenzied and ritual trance. The vision of this tormented genius whirling and storming around his prostrate picture, flinging paint out of cans, waving his arms about, sometimes treading on the canvas himself, sometimes half-running around its perimeter—the thought of this spectacle strikes terribly on the imagination, as we potter so blithely through our Manhattan tour.[1]

But of course Manhattan absorbed and exploited it. Pollock and his colleagues were fast becoming fashionable, and profitable too. The new school was analysed as combining the objectivity of Abstractionism with the subjectivism of Expressionism, and it was given a name, Abstract Expressionism, by Robert Coates the art critic of the *New Yorker*. In all its versions, copies and derivatives it was to make enormous fortunes for Amer-

---

[1] Pollock exhibited his Action Paintings in 1947, becoming one of the first American painters to be internationally recognized in his own lifetime, but only nine years later, aged forty-four, he was killed in a car crash on Long Island.

ican dealers, and was to give the very idea of American art an altogether new ring. Paintings had been big popular business in Manhattan at least since 1942, when Gimbel's and Macy's had both taken to selling great masters (Gimbel's characteristically offering one of its Rembrandts at $9,999). By 1945 Manhattan's forty prewar galleries had multiplied into one hundred fifty, most of them American-owned, some of them frankly decorational: "Important Paintings for Spacious Living" was the title of a showing at the trend-setting Samuel Kootz Gallery. They very soon realized the potential of the New York School—as Elsa Maxwell helpfully wrote in the *New York Post*, "Don't turn down our own artists, no matter how silly or funny you think them." Pollock, de Kooning, Mark Rothko, Robert Motherwell, Adolf Gottlieb and many other local painters were seen now by dealers and consumers alike as highly profitable Manhattan investments.

The chief propagandist of the New York School was not just a dealer, but a patron. The tempestuous millionairess Peggy Guggenheim, lately wife to Max Ernst, had founded her own gallery-museum, Art of the Century, on the top floor of 30 West 57th Street. It was an exhibit in itself, designed by Frederick Kiesler. One of its rooms had walls of gum wood, curved like the walls of a subway station, from which protruded paintings mounted on baseball bats and individually spotlighted. Elsewhere unframed pictures were hung on strings from the ceiling, and the lights went on and off every three seconds. Seven pictures by Paul Klee were mounted on a wheel, which revolved when one crossed a light beam. In this remarkable setting Ms. Guggenheim, herself no slouch at self-projection, presided over the progress of the Abstract Expressionists. She supported Pollock with a monthly stipend, and more astutely than anyone she realized that this was one of those moments in the history of art when a brand new sensibility was emerging from yet another new source, as movements had sprung in the past now from Italy, now from Holland, now from France or Spain.

It was apt that this vulgar, shrewd and perceptive plutocrat, from her provocative midtown gallery, should be presenting to the world a form which seemed to look beyond the exhilaration of the moment, and so often to prefigure, in its whirl of half-controlled chaos, preoccupations of the years to come.[1]

---

[1] Peggy Guggenheim, having founded a far greater museum-gallery in Venice (very rich in Pollocks), died in 1979. Kiesler said that his design for Art of the Century would be remembered longer than the pictures in it, but he was wrong: the floor is now occupied by sober law offices, and when I went up there in 1985 nobody I met had ever heard of the gallery. The political implications of the New York School are explored by Serge Guilbaut in *How New York Stole the Idea of Modern Art*, translated by Arthur Goldhammer (1983). Picasso's *Guernica* was returned to Spain in 1981, General Franco having died at last, and now hangs where it should, in the Prado.

Money

The new profits in art, like new profits in anything, were thoughtfully observed from the towers of the financial district—that second and denser clump of skyscrapers to the south, more froward at least in the mind's eye, less head-in-air than the midtown spectaculars. Manhattan was a manufacturing island—70 percent of all American women's clothing was made there then, together with paper bags, machine tools, dies, packing materials and a hundred other things. The district called The Valley, below Washington Square, was a proper industrial zone, full of small workshops, assembly sheds and union locals.[1] But it was money that Manhattan chiefly made, and money was the prime product down there at the southern end of the island, where the intricate and unpremeditated pattern of building long pre-dated the city's methodical grid. Hidden among those every-which-way blocks was the dark cleft of Wall Street, three centuries before just the northernmost ramparted street of a seashore colony, now a synonym in every language for high finance. The high-walled narrow streets downtown, the sumptuous offices, the scurrying dark-dressed crowds at lunchtime, the es-

---

[1] In the 1960s it became known as SoHo (meaning SOuth of HOuston), and since 1970 its cast-iron factory buildings have been legally leased only to qualified artists, certified by an examining panel and given a card to prove it.

cutcheons of great companies, the sonorous names of banks and stock-brokers—all these were like an inner city within the community of Manhattan, a private powerhouse at the foot of the island.

They were hopeful times, and Wall Street stood, as it well knew, on the brink of most satisfying profits. More overwhelmingly than ever before, Manhattan was the financial capital of America—of the hundred biggest U.S. companies, forty-one had their headquarters here. In 1945 the value of stocks on the New York Stock Exchange rose from $53 billion to $73 billion, and since 1942 the price of a seat there had more than quintupled. Among the bankers, the brokers and the company lawyers the mood was distinctly bullish—the Bankers' Trust booklet spoke for them all. This optimism did not affect, however, the external style of the district, which was extremely cautious and conservative, as though it was still biding its time after the awful shock of 1929. It was very different from the midtown style. The Crash had become in the economic mythology a rival to the Flood or the French Revolution, and the streets and offices of the financial quarter looked for the most part joyless, heavy and very masculine.

Senior financiers and lawyers of Wall Street mostly had British names, and wore British-style clothes, and worked in decors of English affinity. Though their business was the infinitely exciting and risky manipulation of big money, their environment was discreet and un-ostentatious. The partners' room at Brown Brothers Harriman, for instance, a private bank on Wall Street itself, might suggest the consulting rooms of a distinguished but unostentatious Harley Street ear-nose-and-throat specialist: high-ceilinged, that is, sombrely-carpeted, wood-panelled, chandelier'd, with old clocks and open fires and walnut desks and handsome brass fireguards. Even on the floor of the New York Stock Exchange everyone was neatly suited and tied, and inside each broker's booth a gentleman's hat was neatly hung. Wall Street executives had their shoes cleaned, as was traditional, by the row of bootblacks[1] along the churchyard fence of Trinity Church. They lunched, as was customary, at one of the very expensive local clubs— the Downtown Association which had a waiting list seven years long, the Wall Street Club which was decorated with mock-timbering and had high-backed wicker chairs like something from the colonies. When the board of governors of the Stock Exchange met in formal conclave in their noble boardroom, the president on his high dais, his fellow-governors alert and erect on their gilded chairs below, they looked like the cabal of some powerful cult, at seance in their temple. The great law firms of Wall Street were closed societies: it was said to be harder for a Jew to become a partner in one of these institutions than for a black man to join the Ku Klux Klan.

All in all, how stable, how assured! It was hard to realize, from the externals of Wall Street, what a variety of persons really ran this show, queer, clever, bigoted,

---

[1] Now known in Manhattan, I observe, as "shine attendants."

cultivated, ruthless, mingy, kind—what a gamut of personality lay behind the striped suits and the Ivy League accents, from the artistic young David Rockefeller at the Chase National Bank to the scholarly partner at J. P. Morgan whose passion was the mythology and symbolism of the mushroom. (And hard to remember too that only a decade before Wall Street had been in tragic disarray, financiers committing suicide, firms going bankrupt by the score, and an eminent occupant of the Stock Exchange's presidential chair packed off to jail for fraud.)[1]

The Seaport

And now down there at the bottom of the island, after so much meandering and gallivanting, we get to the real point of the city. If we beg a lift in one of those banker's commuting seaplanes, from the seaplane landing at the eastern end of Wall Street, we shall see for ourselves Manhattan's prime and original purpose: to be a seaport. The very word "skyscraper" originally meant the

---

[1] *Life* published a picture feature on Wall Street in January 1946, and its readers' responses were entertaining. One congratulated the magazine on revealing the dehumanized, vulture face of high finance—"not a sag nor a jowl nor a wattle is missing"—while another simply wrote: "It is well to know that the men running our banking institutions look their part—fine-appearing Americans."

topsail of a clipper ship. Navigable channels surrounded Manhattan on all sides; the tide range was a mere four feet, so that ships could berth at any time;[1] the city lay at the fulcrum of a network of bays and waterways, littered with lesser islands and protected from the ocean by the spits of New Jersey and Long Island which all but met out there at the Narrows.

As the little plane banks noisily over our host's office tower, we see the symptoms of a port strewn everywhere around the New York archipelago. To the east are the docks of Brooklyn and the mighty cranes of the navy yard, with the skeleton of an unfinished carrier, perhaps, in the dock below, or the tall grey funnels of a cruiser under refit. To the west wharves and quays, railway sidings and ferry stations straggle along the Jersey shore from Bayonne to Hoboken. To the north a long string of barges is pushing laboriously down the Hudson one way, while up the other the *Clairmont* churns its passage towards Bear Mountain. To the south, beyond the Statue of Liberty, a line of freighters waits for quarantine clearance at the Narrows, and a solitary tanker is sailing, silhouetted against the glitter of the sea, past the Sandy Hook light into the limitless Atlantic.[2]

---

[1] Where I grew up, on the Bristol Channel, the range was forty feet! If we looked the right way, as it happened, there was no land between us and New York harbor, a fact which was one of the excitements of my childhood.

[2] Of which one beloved Manhattan citizen, the stuttering comedian Joe Frisco, observed when somebody commented upon its immensity, "Yeah, and remember we're only seeing the t-t-t-top of it."

All of it, horizon to horizon, seems to be looking inwards to the astonishing island which, like some fantastic encrustation of the tides, stands roaring, flashing and winking in the center. In 1945 the focus of the whole port of New York was Manhattan itself. The island quays were the busiest of all, and as the effects of war receded, and the promises of peace extended themselves, they were about to enter the most prosperous period of their history. The whole world wanted to come to America; half America and its produce wanted to get out into the world; and it was preeminently through this seagate that the traffic was to pass. As our aircraft swings clumsily now up the West Side Highway (oh for a helicopter!) we can see the ocean steamships stacked side by side from the Battery up into the 60s, parked there like trucks in their bays within a few hundred yards of Wall Street or Broadway. Some are already gaudy with the red or yellow smokestacks of the famous shipping companies, some are still shabby with the grey or camouflage of war. They are part of the island's shape, and their protruding angular piers seem to complete the composition of the city, like a decorative frame.

In later years it would be easy to forget that Manhattan was an island at all, let alone a great seaport. In 1945 it was impossible. The skyline was not so dense in those days, so that one could more often see the gleam of water at the end of a street—Cheever's "river light" still bathed the city when the day was right. The winds off the sea seemed closer then. The air was saltier. Besides, there was a Manhattan generation still in its prime which remembered arriving here for the first time, in the climactic moment of its corporate life, upon a ship out of the ocean.

The effects of the port were hard to miss, except in the very center of the island—the procession of the great trucks down to the piers, the deafening coming-and-going of the waterfront, the railway wagons rumbling down to their sidings, the foghorns from the mist, the three farewell hoots of a liner's siren as she cast off from her quay. It was an especially public port. Daily papers carried not only information about ship movements, but also long columns of port news and gossip, often contributed by retired seafarers and rich in anecdote. You could visit the big liners just by asking for a pass at the pierhead, or easily gatecrash their sailing parties—raucous flow of Sherry's champagne in be-flowered crowded staterooms, hilarious opening of telegrams and parting presents, phonograph strains of Benny Goodman clashing down the decks . . . Or at an opposite dockland extreme you could watch the ritual of the shape-up, when longshoremen were picked for work from the crowd of applicants upon the quay: a scene squalid but virile, with its shuffling mass of cloth-capped laborers, the harsh shouts of its officials, and the bitter emptiness that fell upon the scene when all the jobs had been allocated, and the rejected dockers (having failed to pay the necessary kick-backs, perhaps) were left to slope forlornly off.

There were seamen's pubs, brothels, hostels, cafes—the favorite of the transatlantic liner crews was the

Anchor Cafe on 49th Street, which stayed open all night when ships were docked at the neighbouring piers, and greeted its regulars from across the world like members of a club.[1] Some of the grandest of the downtown buildings were sea-structures. On the site of the very first Manhattan house, No. 1 Broadway, stood the splendidly crested offices of the International Mercantile Marine Company, and a few doors away was the Cunard Building, a famously opulent structure decorated, as befitted the customers at its portentous counters, all in gold and marble.[2] India House, an influential club of men connected with the shipping industry in one way or another, described itself as a place "Where Gather Those Who Bear the Burden of the Desert of the Sea": but the burden did not look too onerous, for the club occupied an elegant nineteenth-century mansion in Hanover Square, was handsomely embellished with maritime paintings and ship models, and was rich in retired admirals, cigars and baked clams. The Seamen's Church Institute, a thirteen-story hostel for seamen of all nationalities, was a landmark of the Battery. A figure of Sir Galahad

---

[1] It is now the Olympic Cafe, is still hung around with pictures of ships, and remains popular with the crew of the last of the transatlantic liners, the *QE2*, which docks nearby.

[2] The first is now a Citibank branch, but its doors on Battery Place are still inscribed First Class and Cabin Class; the second is a post office, its domed central space broken up with counters and wooden roofings, its mosaic maps and maritime murals only vestigially to be seen in the gloom above.

stood unexpectedly above its door, illuminated with port and starboard lights, and from the beacon tower above, erected in memory of the *Titanic*, a black time ball fell at noon each day (by which, according to Meyer Berger, elderly tugmen with a distrust of radio signals still preferred to check their chronometers).[1]

An association with the sea carried weight in Manhattan—had not the Vanderbilts themselves begun as ferrymen? The maritime artist Isabella Markell, who had been painting Manhattan shipping scenes since the early 1930s, was a revered figure of the Upper East Side. From her terrace studio near Gracie Mansion she had portrayed hundreds of ships for Navy records during the war, and tug captains would salute her with a plug of the siren as they passed. One of the most highly respected of all city companies was the Moran family tug business, which had been founded in 1863 by an Irish immigrant named Michael Moran. By 1945 it was the world's largest tug company, and its handsome squat-funnelled tugs, all named for members of the Moran family, were inescapable familiars of the waterfront—three long toots of a steam whistle, two short, meant to every shipmaster that a Moran tug was on its way. As perhaps the top tugman of the world the company's chairman, Edmund Moran, had been co-opted in 1944

---

[1] This building was demolished in 1968, but the Titanic Tower was rescued, and today surmounts the information booth at the South Street Seaport Museum. The Institute itself is now in effaced circumstances at 50 Broadway.

as an admiral of the U.S. Navy to arrange the towing of the floating Mulberry harbors for the invasion of Normandy.

And certainly no Manhattan society was more venerated than the Benevolent Association of Sandy Hook Pilots, generally conceded, even by Commodore Sir James Bissett, to be the most skilful of all pilot services. This had its office in one of Manhattan's oldest streets, State Street, and traced its beginnings to the seventeenth century. A Sandy Hook pilot devoted his entire adult life to the service. He spent the first eight years of his career working for his pilot's licence. Then for another seven years he continued his training as a deputy pilot, annually examined, and handling larger and larger ships as time passed. Only after fifteen years of preparation did he become a full-blown, first-rate, absolutely confident, undoubtedly matchless Sandy Hook Pilot—a pilot of pilots in the greatest of all pilot services, whose accident rate was later to be estimated at 89/1000th of one percent ("of which 88 percent," the association's spokesmen claimed, "were of a minor nature"). No wonder these were men of stature. It was a fine sight to see a Sandy Hook pilot, swinging himself across the gap from pilot boat to gang ladder, as he joined a vessel arriving at the Narrows—so assured his leap whatever his age and portliness, so grand a half-swagger up the ladder however often he had done it, and so easy the courtesy with which he received the salute of the officer of the watch above!

The Haven

But you did not need to go out with a pilot boat, did not need a seaplane ride or an invitation to India House, to recognize the consequence and the meaning of this port. You had only to look over the waterways, east or west, for in those days there was almost as much traffic in the harbor as there was on the streets, and billowing black clouds of steamship smoke habitually drifted over the waters. Wherever you looked out there, sea-shapes were moving. There were the strange shapes of floating railway wagons, punted across the East River on scows, and lighters piled with coal or garbage mysteriously propelled by tugs half-hidden in their flanks. There were the tall-stacked saucer-shapes of the ferry steamers, back and forth, back and forth, in and out of those yawning caverns of the ferry stations. There were the buzzing police boats, and the trim pilot launches, and the fire floats, and the graceful *Tourist* and her frumpish sisters loud-speakering their way around the island. There were the last well-worn fishing smacks of Fulton Street. Warships steamed by from the Navy yard, all day long Admiral Moran's formidable tugs—the *Sheila Moran*, the *Margot Moran*, the *Thomas E. Moran*—surged here and there in search of jobs. Two or three fruit ships at a time were often warped into their North River piers beside the Washington Market, and sometimes more than one of the transatlantic liners, too, sailed on the same morning tide from "Liner Row"—Piers 84 to 97: the greatest liners ever built were now resuming their express services to Manhattan, and were about to enter the last magnificent heyday of their history, making this waterfront a glorious place for watching the ships go by.

Such was Manhattan the haven. It was the greatest of all seaports in 1945, but like the city itself it was also an allegory. Even then an immigrant ship occasionally docked on the West Side, and passers-by might glimpse its passengers wide-eyed, shabby-clothed and emaciated from Europe, stumbling through the customs formalities in the echoing arrivals shed: out of the sea like so many before them, bewildered and tongue-tied, but ready to accept, as they stepped with their bags and blankets into the street outside, the island's limitless chance and bounty.[1]

---

[1] Today the maritime business of New York has been dispersed far more widely around the Bay, and many of the Manhattan piers have been obliterated by landfill, depriving the island of its corrugated outline. The peak year for the passenger liners was 1957, and the peak day, September 3, 1957, when twelve liners disembarked 9000 passengers: but in that same year, for the first time, as many people left New York for Europe by air as by sea, and in 1984 the *New York Times* discontinued its daily listing of shipping arrivals and departures. As to the immigrants, for another twenty years they continued to come in ships, but nowadays, like the rest of us, they nearly all reach their haven out of the skies.

Epilogue

I CHOSE the title *Manhattan '45* because it sounded partly like a kind of gun, and partly like champagne, and thus matched the victorious and celebratory theme of my book. But like bubbles and victories, that moment of release, pride and happiness was not to last.

I suppose we have been seeing, in this laughing and self-congratulatory place, the American idea on the brink of its middle age. Postwar Manhattan has seemed to me a late epitome of a more youthful America, recognizably inspired still by the aspirations of its Founding Fathers—tolerance, self-reliance, opportunity and a constitutional right to the pursuit of happiness. Its citizens still worshipped gods, as Cheever was to say, "as ancient as yours and mine," and I think most people, looking back on the island city then, without forgetting its faults and miseries, would declare it all in all, as cities go, a good and merry place.

Inevitably it changed. The world caught up with its goodness and its merriment. Very soon the nuclear bomb was to be seen not as the guarantor of peace, but as the instrument of annihilation. Within a few years the sensations of Manhattan had shifted, the euphoria had subsided; the island, like the nation, was becoming graver, more difficult, less sure of itself. In 1946 Churchill invented the Iron Curtain, and the Americans were plunged into their Cold War against the Russians. Network TV arrived, altering the habits, the tastes and the values of New York. The International Style fell upon its architecture, tempering the gaudy exuberance. By 1949 the economic boom was faltering, crime was mounting, and E. B. White could write that the city "had never been so uncomfortable, so crowded, so tense."[1] Worse was to come, too—the fearful spread of drug addiction, the trauma of national humiliation, municipal near-bankruptcy and a general slow decline into cynicism.

It was to be expected. Out of the delight of 1945 another city had emerged. Manhattan had not merely become the chief metropolis of the greatest power, but

---

[1] In his essay *Here Is New York*, evoking what its blurb nevertheless still called "the greatest town in the world—the gaudiest, most beautiful, most crowded, most private, most satisfying, most heartbreaking city in all history."

actually the nearest thing there had ever been to a world capital, with the offices of the United Nations down on the East River where the slaughterhouses had been. Age began to show, but not only age—maturity, too. Before very long Manhattan would begin to seem to some visitors a trifle old-fashioned, but this was only the patina of experience. You cannot be a Wonder City for ever, you grow out of the brag and the dazzle, you no longer care much if Chicago has a taller building, Tokyo faster escalators, Montreal better subways. A little of the impetuous pride left the place. New Yorkers no longer claimed that in Manhattan anything was possible, boasted about feeding Europe's poor with the civic garbage, or even perhaps walked down Fifth Avenue with quite the boxer's truculence of Tom Buchanan.

Yet this island was to remain one of the glories of civilization. Muggers might prowl Central Park, but a new flood of immigrants came in, from every corner of the world now, to confirm the city's first and noblest function; and still it was possible, wandering through these streets in the warm of a summer evening, say, with Manhattan's life and hope and color in swarming vigor all around you, to laugh out loud at the happiness of being you. If ever nuclear war were unleashed upon the world this city would doubtless be among the first to go; but even its ruins might prove to whoever came after what splendour men and women could achieve at their best, and what fun they sometimes had achieving it.

All this we see in retrospect, like a swell riding up-river from the prow of the *Queen* as she sailed in such triumph through the Bay. The men who crowded her decks had brought Manhattan new greatness by their victory, and enlarged its destiny. They had left behind them, however, many comrades who would never experience this fulfillment for themselves. The next day's *New York Times*, carrying joyful pictures of the liner's arrival, quoting Captain Astheimer about his reserves of Morale Maintenance Girls and telling the story of the nurse and her black lace underwear, also reported the deaths in action of nine young men from New York itself: and it is to their memory, since they cannot be here to sail into port with us today, that I have dedicated this book.

Acknowledgements

THIS ENTIRE WORK is really an acknowledgement, because
it is meant to express my gratitude for thirty-three years of
bewitched association with New York—I have visited the
city every year, written many thousands of words about it,
and made there some of my oldest and truest friendships.
More specifically I should say thank you to all the people
who have helped me imagine the place as it was in 1945,
to the authors (named in my text) of other books I have
quoted, to my editor Stephanie Sakson-Ford, and to the
staffs of the two libraries, those of the New-York Historical
Society and the New York Society, that I have chiefly used.

But most of all I thank—Manhattan!

Trefan Morys, 1987   J.M.